Schaum's Quick Guide
to Great Business Writing

Other Books in Schaum's Quick Guide Series

Forthcoming titles:

Schaum's Quick Guide to Writing Great Short Stories
Schaum's Quick Guide to Great Presentation Skills
Schaum's Quick Guide to Writing Great Essays
Schaum's Quick Guide to Great Research Papers

Schaum's Quick Guide to Great Business Writing

How to Write Letters, Papers, Memos, and Job Applications

Suzanne Sparks FitzGerald

McGraw-Hill

New York   San Francisco   Washington, D.C.   Auckland   Bogotá
Caracas   Lisbon   London   Madrid   Mexico City   Milan
Montreal   New Delhi   San Juan   Singapore
Sydney   Tokyo   Toronto

Library of Congress Cataloging-in-Publication Data

FitzGerald, Suzanne Sparks.
    Schaum's quick guide to great business writing / Suzanne Sparks
FitzGerald.
        p.   cm.   —   (Schaum's quick guide series)
    Includes index.
    ISBN 0-07-022060-3
    1. Business writing—Handbooks, manuals, etc.   I. Title.
II. Series.
HF5718.3.F56   1998
808'.06665—dc21   98-31564
                                                                         CIP

McGraw-Hill

A Division of The **McGraw·Hill** Companies

4 5 6 7 8 9 10 DOC/DOC 0 9 8 7 6 5 4 3

ISBN 0-07-022060-3

*The sponsoring editor for this book was Barbara Gilson, the editing supervisor was Fred
Dahl, the designer was Inkwell Publishing Services, and the production supervisor was
Tina Cameron. It was set in Stone Serif by Inkwell Publishing Services.*

Printed and bound by R. R. Donnelley & Sons Company.

McGraw-Hill books are available at special quantity discounts to use as premiums
and sales promotions, or for use in corporate training sessions. For more information, please write to the Director of Special Sales, McGraw-Hill, 11 West 19th
Street, New York, NY 10011. Or contact your local bookstore.

This book is printed on recycled, acid-free paper containing
a minimum of 50% recycled, de-inked fiber.

Dedicated to Baby Fitz

Contents

Preface   ix

PART I READABLE WRITING   **1**

Chapter 1—Know Your Audience   3

Chapter 2—What Should Your Writing Do?   17

Chapter 3—The Power of Words to Express, Not Impress   25

PART II WORKING ON STRUCTURE AND STYLE   **43**

Chapter 4—Easy Formats to Guide Your Reader   45

Chapter 5—The Power of Visuals, White Space, and Headings   63

Chapter 6—How to Start and Stop   81

Chapter 7—Brush Up on Your Grammar   93

Chapter 8—Using Action Verbs   115

PART III SITUATIONAL WRITING   **127**

    Chapter 9—Delivering Bad News   129

    Chapter 10—Writing for Martians   139

POSTSCRIPT: DO'S AND DON'TS—THE FINAL CHECKLIST   151

    Index   159

Preface

Most of us wouldn't try to build a house without the knowledge of how to use raw materials and tools like lumber, nails, and a hammer. But many of us try to write without fully understanding our most basic tool—words. Writers use words much like carpenters use lumber, nails, and a hammer: They cut, shape, and form them into products like letters, reports, and e-mail.

Our words also need structure or grammar much like a house needs a frame. If we know how to use grammar, a concrete writing tool, we can write more effectively just as a carpenter uses a frame to build a well structured house.

We might not all be expert craftspeople yet, but we can learn techniques and formats to become more skilled. That's why I wrote this book—for students and managers smart enough to realize the value of effective writing.

According to surveys of employers worldwide, writing grammatically correct, easy-to-read, informative, and persuasive information tops the list of skills needed for professional success. And so the three sections of this guide attempt to provide you with the tools to hone this top-ranked skill.

Part I of this *Quick Guide* discusses readable writing and how to craft your letters, reports, and e-mail to convey important information to readers or to persuade them of your concerns or issues.

Part II talks about the structure and style of your writing and presents easy formats to convince readers to both start and continue reading your important messages.

Part III addresses several difficult writing situations such as writing for those with limited knowledge of the content or writing instructions for actual users or delivering bad news.

This guide includes many exercises and examples so that you can practice using the writing tools available to you. The postscript summarizes all the tips this book provides and offers a final checklist for those who choose to become expert craftspeople of their language. I hope you are one of them!

Suzanne Sparks FitzGerald

Schaum's Quick Guide
to Great Business Writing

Part I

Readable Writing

Chapter 1

Know Your Audience

Speak "Right" to the Crowd

To succeed academically and professionally you must communicate well, particularly in writing. Often, you must forget what your high school English teachers taught you and write in a simpler, more direct way.

To write effectively, you must know your audience. The more you know, the easier it is to tailor or customize your message for an individual or group.

You might compare the style of your writing to clothing. While a college English paper may call for a jacket and tie, an internal memo might argue for a T-shirt and jeans. Your job as a writer is to achieve a certain effect on your readers. If you want to have the greatest effect, adjust your style to suit the audience. Just as you shouldn't go underdressed to a job interview, you shouldn't overdress either. Wearing a white tie and tails would make you look ridiculous at a barbecue. You must figure out what your audience expects. The careful writer takes the time to discover what works best for each audience.

First, visualize the person or persons you write to or for most frequently. Whom do you need to persuade or inform— your professor or your manager?

Investigate your audience as part of the writing process. If you can discover information such as age, educational level, income, and gender, you will write more appropriately. If you can determine interests, opinions, and values, you can speak "right" to the crowd. You need to uncover your reader's knowledge of your topic: Is he an expert? Does she know anything about your subject?

It's Helpful to Know

- Age, education, income, gender
- Interests, opinions, values
- Reader's knowledge of your topic

A Web page designed for college students tried to arouse a sense of activism in the students; unfortunately, the Web page referred to activists like Ralph Nader, whose names the students didn't recognize.

A direct mail piece with a gun control message sent to a National Rifle Association audience caused the audience to feel more vehemently opposed to gun control.

An environmental services brochure sent to purchasing managers used such technical language that the confused purchasers chose another source.

In the first example, the writer didn't consider the age of the audience. In the gun control example, the values of the audience were ignored. In the third example, the writer didn't consider the reader's knowledge of the topic.

What If You Don't Know Your Audience?

You have fifteen minutes to write a memo and you don't know much about the audience you will address. Spend a few minutes determining which of the categories described in the Audience Types box most closely fits your reader. Then you can easily adjust your writing.

EXPERTS VS. BOTTOM-LINERS

Try to evaluate whether your reader is a layperson, expert, executive, user, or complex audience type. Once you categorize your reader, try this list of do's and don'ts.

A **layperson** has little expertise in a subject matter. Therefore, laypeople usually have no particular motivation to read your letter. As an effective writer you must motivate or attract your reader. Starting with a benefit helps. A layperson is not knowledgeable about your subject; therefore, you must adjust your tone, style, and vocabulary.

For example, if you must write to employees about various health care plans, find an interesting fact or a reason (benefit) for them to read your first paragraph, such as how they can receive 100 percent coverage for dependents.

DO: Find a way to attract attention.
DON'T: Bore your reader with detail.

Example:
A person who uses a computer but does not know any software program well.

An **expert** cares about process and detail. If you were writing a paper describing a chemistry experiment, for example, a chemist would want to know how to reproduce your results by reading about all the procedures you followed. Give experts the specifics. The same detail would scare or bore the layperson.

For example, if you write to an expert in health care benefits, spell out the details of the policy. The expert will understand and appreciate the specifics.

DO: Focus on procedure or process.
DON'T: Only give bottom-line data.

Example:
A computer scientist who writes software programs and wants to know how you developed a particular program.

An **executive** audience wants bottom-line information. Detailed descriptions that work for experts do not work for this audience. Use straightforward language and tone. Provide the benefits and the needed information first.

For example, give the executive audience a summary of the health care benefits package in one paragraph or less, then proceed with other important points.

DO: Get to the point.
DON'T: Explain in detail.

Example:
The manager in charge of selling the software product who doesn't care how it works, but needs to know how to sell it.

The **user** must carry out your instructions; for example, the user of a software package must read your documentation in order to do a job. This person doesn't care how you wrote the software package or about the process, but only how to make it work.

The user in our health care benefits example needs to follow the complicated medical benefits policy. Help the employee-user by explaining clearly how to use the benefits.

DO: Realize this person might not know as much as you do.
DON'T: Be too brief.

Example:
The person who must use the software and understand how to make it work.

Adapting your writing to a **complex** reader is more difficult. An example is a layperson/executive, a manager with no particular expertise in your field. Suppose that this person serves as your supervisor and you must motivate him to read your work. Use benefits to catch his attention and a bottom-line style to keep his interest.

You might report to an **expert/executive,** an engineer who has worked her way up in the company to become CEO. An executive summary followed by a detailed explanation will work for this CEO.

An **expert/user** needs to know how the process works and how he can implement it. A communication manager who still writes and edits newsletters is an example of an expert/user.

A **layperson/user**—for example, an employee using the Internet—needs motivation and information. With no particular expertise or information, this person may have difficulty accessing E-mail messages.

Sometimes you will write for a **mixed** audience, meaning that your readers comprise all five audience types. When writing a company newsletter you must address laypeople, experts, executives, users, and complex audience types. In this case, you must write for the lowest common denominator, or the layperson.

Exercise:

Identify the person or group you write to or for most frequently. What can you do to adjust to this specific audience type?

Layperson_____

Expert_____

Executive_____

User_____

Complex_____

Mixed_____

Exercise:

In the following exercise try writing about the same subject for four different audiences. Note the differences!

Challenge Topic: *How to deal with an angry customer*

Audience 1: **Layperson** (a 12-year-old boy)
Adjust your vocabulary and tone to fit the audience. In a memo or E-mail message, tell the boy how he should deal with an angry customer on his paper route.

Audience 2: **Expert** (a college English professor who will grade your writing)
Again, adjust your vocabulary and tone. Explain to the professor how you would deal with an angry customer or how she might deal with an angry student.

Audience 3: **Executive** (a prospective employer who will use this writing sample to evaluate your writing skills)
Keep in mind the bottom-line orientation of this audience.

Audience 4: **User** (a friend or peer)
Tell your friend or peer how you might handle a difficult customer and what steps your friend might take to achieve good results.

Notice that even though the subject is the same, the approaches differ for each audience type. Try it again with a different subject:

Challenge Topic: *How to select a college major*
Use the same four audience types.

Audience 1: **Layperson** (a high school junior)
Adjust your vocabulary and tone to fit the audience. In a memo or E-mail message, tell the student how to select a potential college major.

Audience 2: **Expert** (a college English professor who will grade your writing)
Again, adjust your vocabulary and tone. Explain to the professor how you would choose a college major.

Audience 3: **Executive** (a prospective employer who will use this writing sample to evaluate your writing skills)
Keep in mind the bottom-line orientation of this audience.

Audience 4: **User** (a friend or peer)
Tell your friend or peer how you would choose a major and how she might select one also.

Suggested Responses:

Here's how one writer completed the first exercise:

Challenge Topic: *How to deal with an angry customer*

Layperson (a 12-year-old newspaper delivery boy)

> Dear Steven:
>
> If Mr. Smith was mad at you, maybe you did something wrong. Doesn't he like his newspaper by the front door? When any of the people on your paper route get mad, tell them you are sorry.
>
> Ask the person what you did wrong. Then try not to do it again. Try to make your customers happy.

Note the simple vocabulary and informal tone.

Expert (an advertising manager for a daily newspaper)

> Dear Nancy:
>
> When I deal with an angry customer, I try to understand the root of his or her dissatisfaction. As you know, a happy customer generally doesn't talk about a good experience, but an angry customer reaches a large audience base.
>
> It is difficult to deal with a hostile customer because the complaint may not be justified. Still, I find it imperative to listen with empathy, restate the problem, agree on a solution or next step, and confirm that the proposed solution meets the customer's need.

Note the emphasis on how the writer solved problems and the explanation of the process.

Executive (a sales manager for the newspaper)

> Dear Scott:
>
> We have an angry customer on our hands. I suggest we immediately address the problem and resolve it as revenues could be negatively affected if we don't. I'm not sure what happened, but we need to reestablish goodwill and satisfy this complaint.

Note the emphasis on the bottom line and the direct approach.

User (customer service representative for the newspaper)

> Dear Valerie:
>
> As our customer service representative, you must reestablish goodwill with our key customer. I'm not sure why he is so irritated with us. Please find out what the problem is and resolve it in the most expedient way.
>
> I don't have to tell you how important this account is to us. I suggest agreeing with the customer that there is a significant problem, promising to avoid such a conflict in the future, and ensuring we satisfy the customer with the solution. Thanks for your help.

Note that Valerie must deal with the angry customer; tell her what to do.

Learn Your Fog Index

Writing for your audience also includes knowing its knowledge level; writing for a student is not the same as writing for a professor. Find out who you are writing for and tailor your message, tone, and purpose accordingly.

Determining your fog index is a way to know whether you generally write for high school graduates or Ph.D.'s.

You can determine your Gunning-Mueller Fog Index™ by following these easy steps:

- Find the average sentence length of a 100-word sample of your writing.
- Find the number of words with three or more syllables in your sample without counting proper nouns.
- Add these two figures and multiply the sum by .4 to find your fog index. That index is the reading grade level at which the copy was written. (A score of 12 equals high school graduate level, 16 equals college graduate level, 19 or higher equals Ph.D. level.)

Compare your index with the sophistication of your audience and then rewrite if necessary. Here's an example from a previous version of this chapter.

Sample

Knowing your audience might be the most critical factor in effective writing. The more you know, the easier it is to tailor or customize your message for an individual or group.
Sometimes all you know is that your audience has a short attention span. Read on for how to address **[50 words]** that audience.
I once wrote a report for 18-year-old readers. I referred to a classic musical, *My Fair Lady*; unfortunately, this group was too young and had no idea what I was talking about. I lost credibility and the attention of my audience.
If you know demographics, psychographics, lifestyle **[100 words]** factors, and management style, you can dramatically increase your ability to inform or persuade your audience.

- Count the number of words in each sentence and divide by the number of sentences; 100 words divided by eight sentences equals 12.5.
- Next, count the number of words of three or more syllables. I found 17 words with three or more three syllables.
- Add 12.5 and 17 and multiply by .4. I wrote the sample at 11.8, or a high school graduate level.

If you write on too high or too low a level for your reader, your audience will probably find your writing either difficult to understand or insulting. Most newspapers in the USA use a 12-year-old reading level.

Exercise:

Use a 100-word sample of your writing and find your Fog Index. Now you know whether you write for grade school students or nuclear physicists.

_____

_____

_____

_____

_____

_____

_____

_____

_____

_____

Now that you know your audience and at what level you write, how do you attract your reader?

"You" Versus "Me"

Feature the "you attitude" and benefits to your audience. Many audiences are hostile, or neutral at best. Readers want to know what's in it for them. Why should they read your E-mail message, memo, letter, or report? How will reading your document benefit them?

When answering a complaint letter, in many instances you face a hostile audience. If you start out with why the reader is wrong and you are right, you'll lose your audience before you start. You could start by finding some common ground or agreeing with the audience on a particular point or issue. Agreeing with your readers tends to disarm them and they become open to persuasion.

Many writers feature the "me" attitude. I have included some paragraphs from cover letters with this attitude. It's hard to persuade an audience. Featuring the "me" attitude may condemn your masterpiece to the trash can.

Exercise:

Using these excerpts from actual letters, rewrite the sentences with a "reader" or "you" attitude.

1. Although I would seem to be enormously overqualified for your position, I invite you to consider using my services.
2. I read your ad for communications writer and said to myself, "This job is perfect for me."
3. I'm writing to request that you do not hire me as a part-time writer. Instead, use me as a consultant.
4. I'm at your service if this matter is worth discussing.
5. I am looking for interesting, part-time work.
6. I live less than 15 minutes from your office, which is convenient for me.
7. I would like to work for a firm like yours.
8. I enjoyed talking with you on the phone about my proposal.
9. I have investigated this subject at length and would like to report it all here.
10. I'm taking this course because it is required.
11. Did I miss anything at the meeting yesterday?
12. I am interested in getting started in the design field and would like to start with your firm.
13. I would like to work for SKF Industries because I am an engineer.
14. This subject is of great interest to me.

Possible Answers:

1. My years of experience in the data processing arena could benefit your company.

2. I'm responding to your advertisement for a communications writer. I would like to put my writing expertise to work for your company.

3. I would like you to consider hiring me as a part-time writer. My consulting experience will benefit your company in the following ways.

4. I would like to meet with you soon to discuss your exciting opportunity.

5. Perhaps I could fill your need for a part-time worker.

6. Your location is so convenient, I would have no trouble arriving on time, even in bad weather.

7. My experience and education could benefit your firm.

8. My proposal could help you cut costs and increase productivity.

9. My research indicates the following five items you might need to know.

10. This required course addresses many important facets of my career.

11. What did you cover at the meeting yesterday?

12. I'd like to put my training to work for your firm.

13. My engineering skills could benefit SKF Industries in the following ways....

14. I think you'll find this subject fascinating.

Using the "you" attitude captures the attention of readers. How do you, the writer, maintain that reader interest? Try building rapport with your audience.

Build Reader Rapport

What should you do for the audience with a short attention span? In some ways, a hostile audience is similar to the audience with a short attention span. You may write to hostile audiences frequently—readers who oppose you, your ideas, or your topic. If you represent a student group and must ask (beg) the Student Government Association for more money, you may face a hostile or uninterested audience.

Most audiences have a short attention span because of lack of time or an overload of obligations. Try the following tips to build rapport with readers who have a short attention span or may oppose your ideas:

- Establish common ground. Bond with the audience to dispel hostility. Appeal to the reader's needs or interests.
- Agree with readers if you know their position. At least acknowledge the reader's position and recognize valid objections to your view.
- Attract attention with a reader benefit. What will the reader gain from reading your ideas?
- Use short paragraphs to hold interest. Keep your evidence clear and dispel any objections the audience may hold.
- Feature the "you" attitude. Don't hammer away at your position; keep the focus on your audience.

Now that you've established rapport with the audience, keep in mind the use of nonsexist language. If you offend readers, they may not get past your first paragraph.

Try Nonsexist Language

Sexist language, in addition to offending some, may also mislead the reader because it may be ambiguous. When writing, avoid using *him/her* or *she/he*; instead use the plural *they*, which the reader will find less cumbersome and easier to understand. English does not have a neuter tense, so it's difficult to always use politically correct pronouns. The best option is to use the plural. When possible, avoid offending any audience member.

Examples:

1. An employee should consider *his/her* options before signing the waiver.

or

Employees should consider *their* options before signing the waiver.

2. The manager in charge of selling the software product doesn't care how it works, but how *he/she* will sell it.

or

Managers in charge of selling the software product don't care how it works, but how *they* will sell it.

Exercise:

Try creating gender-neutral terms for the following examples:

Sexist language	Gender-neutral language
mailman	_____
congressman	_____
chairman	_____
stewardess	_____
spokesman	_____
layman	_____
repairman	_____
fireman	_____
salesman	_____
beautician	_____
policeman	_____
deliveryman	_____
manpower	_____
mankind	_____
manmade	_____
manhours	_____
freshman	_____
forefathers	_____
foreman	_____
coed	_____

Possible Answers:

mail carrier, congressperson, chairperson, flight attendant, spokesperson, layperson, repairperson, fire fighter, salesperson, stylist, police officer, delivery person, workforce, humankind, manufactured, work hours, first-year student, ancestors, supervisor, student

The following checklist will help you to speak "right" to the crowd. Follow these simple tips to quickly improve your writing.

Checklist: Speak "Right" to the Crowd

- Find out as much as possible about your reader.
- Use a "you" attitude.
- When in doubt, write clearly, for a 12-year-old reader.
- Motivate a layperson to read.
- Feature a detailed process for an expert.
- Use the bottom line for an executive audience.
- Tell user audiences how to do it.
- For a complex audience (an individual who fits more than one category), combine audience types.
- For a mixed audience, write to laypeople.
- Remember, all readers want to know what's in it for them.
- Whenever possible, use nonsexist language.

Chapter 2

What Should Your Writing Do?

Know Your Purpose

Do you want to inform or persuade your reader? Do you need to teach or record an activity? Research proves that it is more effective to have one objective or purpose than many.

Remember your purpose as you write. I once had a professor who wrote, "So what?" at the end of some of my papers. If you ask yourself the "So what?" question and you cannot answer it, then your readers will experience the same problem.

Some Purposes of Professional and Business Writing

- Inform.
- Persuade.
- Teach.
- Record or document.

Exercise:

See if you can match the following examples to a purpose.

Example 1: ❑ Inform ❑ Persuade ❑ Teach ❑ Document

We provide the most cost-effective solution of any of our competitors. We have the expertise, the personnel, and the resources to design a state-of-the-art day care center for you.

We can increase your productivity and decrease absenteeism by providing this on-site day care center at a competitive price.

Consider carefully the following benefits of choosing our firm: increased productivity, improved employee morale, decreased absenteeism, decreased tardiness, and the knowledge that you have selected the premier provider of day care services.

Example 2: ❏ Inform ❏ Persuade ❏ Teach ❏ Document

TO: Great Valley Personnel
FROM: Quality Improvement Team
SUBJECT: Parking Lot Lights
DATE: June 20, 1998

Additional lights will be installed on the perimeter of the parking lot this summer. There will be a total of 11 new lights, three in each side lot and five along the back lot.

These lights should create a safer environment. If you have any questions, call any member of the quality team. Enjoy!

Example 3: ❏ Inform ❏ Persuade ❏ Teach ❏ Document

TO: Human Resources
FROM: Bruce Bratz
DATE: March 6, 1998
RE: Order Entry Problems

On March 6, 1998, Bruce Bratz met with Wendy Catlett to discuss her order entry errors. After evaluating Wendy's errors, Bruce found no particular pattern to her incidents. He suggested having an experienced customer service representative sit with her to actively monitor her customer service skills.

Wendy is considered a good customer representative who achieves the 55 percent availability ratio. Bruce found Wendy receptive to his suggestions; she hopes to reduce her order entry errors.

Example 4: ❏ Inform ❏ Persuade ❏ Teach ❏ Document

Welcome to your Mr. Espresso Machine! In order to use this product properly, you must follow some simple directions. If you follow the directions, you will enjoy a delicious cup of espresso or cappuccino.

1. Have a stainless steel container to froth milk.
2. Make sure your machine is plugged in.
3. Place the appropriate amount of espresso in the dispenser shown in Figure 1.

4. Be careful not to touch the machine while brewing.
5. Froth milk by inserting the plastic cable into the stainless steel container.
6. Enjoy with your favorite topping.

Answers:

Example 1 **persuades** us because of its reader benefits, tone, and vocabulary. Example 2 **informs** us because it provides straightforward information rather than instruction or a persuasive message. Example 3 **documents** or records Wendy's problem and Bruce's conversation with her. Example 4 is an owner's manual designed to **teach** the buyer how to use the product.

Once you've determined your purpose, the writing process can begin.

Writing versus Rewriting

Planning saves time later in the writing process. If you clearly outline your purpose and content, you'll spend less time revising and editing later. Just as a good presentation requires a plan or outline, so does a well-written E-mail message, memo, letter, or report. Most writers write and edit; few plan and revise. Four helpful steps in the writing process include: planning, writing, revising, and editing.

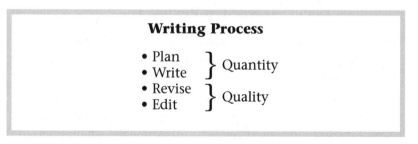

Writing Process

- Plan
- Write } Quantity
- Revise
- Edit } Quality

PLANNING AND WRITING

In the planning stage, you may need to brainstorm. An outline will ensure that you organize your materials in a meaningful way. If you plan and format your writing, your organization will be apparent to your reader.

The planning and writing stages are quantity steps: It's easier to edit a full page than a blank one. In both the planning and writing stages, strive for volume. Don't worry about quality; try to produce a lengthy piece.

The revision and editing stages are quality steps to ensure that everything is as you intended. CEOs complain that employees don't revise or edit E-mail messages, thus embarrassing themselves and the company by using poor grammar or allowing careless errors to remain uncorrected.

REVISION AND EDITING

Many people confuse revision with editing. Revision employs the "cut and paste" method of moving, removing, and adding additional copy. For example, the paragraph on page 3 might work better on page 5. Revision also includes deleting unnecessary paragraphs or adding detail to an explanation.

Editing, the final step in the revision process, involves examining the accuracy, spelling, and grammar of your E-mail message, memo, or report.

Five-Step Revision

A thorough revision consists of five steps. You might not need this process for an E-mail message, but try it for a long report.

Five-Step Revision

- Overall purpose and content: The "so what" question.
- Overall structure and organization: Does it make sense in this order?
- Paragraph level accuracy: Is each paragraph complete?
- Sentence level accuracy: Does each sentence make sense?
- Your personal grammatical errors: What problems do you have?

First, read your written piece only for purpose and content; decide whether your content makes sense and your purpose seems clear.

Second, look at how you organized the report; does the section on page 3 fit well there? Compare your report to your outline or table of contents to see whether you organized the information in the best way.

Third, look at each paragraph to see whether each sentence belongs where it is and whether the information makes sense grouped in that way.

Fourth, look at each sentence to make sure there are no sentence fragments or run-on sentences.

Last, read for personal grammatical errors, looking for those errors you most commonly make, like switching verb tense or misusing possessive pronouns or commas. Most people regularly commit some type of grammatical error. Make sure to read the entire piece one final time, blocking out everything but that personal error.

Editing tests your quality. Check for misspellings or double words. Examine your grammar and spelling. Have someone else edit your work, particularly someone who knows your weaknesses.

Exercise:

Try revising and editing the following short articles. They are both wordy, hard to follow, and filled with grammatical errors.

Privacy in the Workplace

You will need to produce explanations for monitoring of communications in a wide variety of communications in the office including: conversations on the telephone, written letters and computer disk files.

And similar rationale must be presented to defend against searches of desks, filing cabinets, briefcases and purses.

Once you have established a policy stating that "all communications are subject to monitoring by management," should you then listen to personal phone calls, and survey personnel.

"I do not advise listening in to personal calls," says Stevenson. "there are common law rights of privacy among the states to consider. A court may well ask 'why did you decide to listen to the conversation'"?

Note that some states have laws that explicitly deny employers the right to listen in on personal phone calls. Check with your attorney.

_____

_____

_____

_____

_____

_____

_____

_____

_____

_____

_____

_____

_____

_____

_____

_____

_____

Terminating an Employee

One method of avoiding litigation is to offer the employee compensation in return for the employees' waiver of his or her right to sue the employer. But courts will not enforce such arrangements that are not bargained-for exchanges. In other words, the employee who waives his or her right to sue, must get, in return, something beyond that to which they already are entitled.

Employees also must have adequate time to review the waiver. Outplacement services are offered by some employers as a means of helping terminated employees think about the future, instead of dwelling on what has just occurred. Outplacement firms which assist the employee in finding a new job, usually charge a percentage of what the employee made, commonly 15 percent if the employee was upper management.

_____

_____

_____

_____

_____

_____

_____

_____

_____

_____

_____

_____

_____

_____

_____

_____

Possible Rewrites:

Privacy in the Workplace

Employers must explain their rationale for monitoring workplace communications such as phone calls, letters, and electronic mail, as well as their rationale for searches of desks, filing cabinets, or briefcases and purses.

Stevenson addressed the question of whether you should listen to personal calls or conduct employee surveys by noting common law rights of privacy. Some state laws deny employers the right to listen to personal phone calls. Check with your attorney before taking any action.

Terminating an Employee

If you must terminate employees, you can often avoid litigation by offering compensation in return for the employees' waiving their rights to sue you. Employees must receive adequate time to review the waiver, as well as additional compensation of some kind.

Some employers offer outplacement services to terminated employees. The outplacement firms typically charge the employer 15 percent of the most recent salary for upper management employees and a flat fee for other employees.

Try the following checklist ideas to ensure your writing accomplishes what you want it to do.

Checklist: What Should Your Writing Do?

- Know your single purpose or objective.
- Adjust your style, tone, and vocabulary to inform, persuade, teach, or record.
- Plan and revise your writing; don't just write and edit.
- Consider a five-step revision.
- Determine your personal grammatical problems and look for them.

Chapter 3

The Power of Words to Express, Not Impress

Sometimes writers use words to impress, not to express. When we use words that impress, our audience might not understand us. We might write at a very high fog index, which could impress ourselves as writers or even impress readers, if they can understand us. But writing to express focuses our attention on the reader, not the writer.

Now that we know how to identify the audience and how to determine our purpose, we must craft our words in an expressive, readable way.

Feature Clarity, Economy, and Straightforwardness

Readability has many facets, but the most important are clarity, economy, and straightforwardness. *Clarity* is the opposite of ambiguity. If your writing is unclear, the reader can't be sure what you mean. In business or professional writing, you must ensure that the reader understands your message. *Economy*, or using no more words than necessary, distinguishes clear and forceful writing from long-winded prose. Become familiar with the "Delete Word" option on your word processor. *Straightforwardness* refers to the order in which you write, placing the subject close to the verb for easy understanding.

If your message has more than one meaning, it is not clear. Don't use long words when short ones will do; it makes your writing dense and difficult to understand. Words ending in *-ality, -ize, -ization, -ational,* and so on make sentences more complex than necessary. For example, *drama* works better than *dramatization* and *functional* works better than *functionality.* Use precision to make your writing clear. Make sure the words you choose have exactly the right (and only one) meaning. Use specific words. Don't say *organization* if you mean *the American Red Cross.* Don't use *situation* if you mean *layoff.*

Learn to revise sentences so they become clear and unambiguous.

Example:

1. My educational background basically centers around a B.A. in business administration as an economics major.

2. I spent two quarters studying the stock market and three quarters of finance which will allow me to handle your financial accounts.

The first sentence confuses the reader: Do you or don't you hold a degree? The phrase *centers around* should be avoided. In the second example, what do the quarters mean? Three months? Ten weeks? If the information you offer is negative, omit it. Why say you've only studied the stock market for twenty weeks? Why not rephrase the unclear sentences like this:

1. I hold a B.A. in economics.

2. My experience studying the stock market and finance will benefit your accounts.

You can make your writing as clear as possible by deleting words that don't add meaning. Avoid the meaningless modifiers in this list:

actually	kind of
basically	particular
certain	practically
definitely	really
different	various

26

generally	very
given	virtually
individual	

Example:

Actually, I *generally* enjoy typing *practically* any *specific* type of communication.

The italicized modifiers weaken the sentence.

ECONOMY

Most business writers use a 17-word rule when writing sentences. You always want to vary the length of your sentences; however, if you use too many words you may lose readers. They might get to the end of a lengthy sentence and not remember how it started.

If your message is delivered in long, arduous prose, no one may read it. Economy refers both to the number of words in a sentence and to the lack of redundant phrases or words. Active writing reduces the number of words you use.

The following example illustrates a sentence that is so long that when you finish reading it, you'll forget how it started.

Seller shall hold harmless ABC against, and shall handle and defend against any claim, suit or other proceeding brought against ABC based on an allegation that any software, design, service and or other materials (property) provided to ABC pursuant to this contract constitutes an infringement or material breach of any United States patent, copyright or other proprietary information right, provided that Seller is notified in writing of such allegation, suit or proceeding and given full and complete authority, information and assistance (at Seller's expense) for the defense of same. (*89 words*)

Unfortunately, some of our sentences look like the previous example and make the reader's life miserable. Try your hand at changing these sentences.

Exercise:

Revise these sentences for economy.

1. In order to facilitate accomplishment of minimization of disruption or crippling of work effort and wastage of man-hours resul-

tant from this activity, immediate effectuation of the following
procedures is hereby announced.

_____

_____

_____

2. Parking in the lot adjacent to the building will be restricted by
space allocation designation for workmens' vehicles and the four
outermost spaces will be reserved for foremen of the construction crew so employees should make other arrangements for
parking during that time frame and consider implementation of
vehicular co-transportation.

Source: Michael Keene's *Effective Business Writing*

_____

_____

_____

First, what content in the sentence is necessary for reader understanding? Can you eliminate unnecessary phrases
and redundancies? Possible rewrites follow:

1. To carry on work as usual, follow these procedures.
2. Consider carpooling because parking next to the building is primarily for construction workers.

Wordiness. Using wordy phrases tends to confuse the
reader. According to Gary Provost in *Writer's Digest*, when you
use too many adjectives you leave your reader gasping for
breath. Try to practice spotting wordy phrases and correcting
them. In the next exercise, use one word to replace several.

Exercise:

Find a one-word substitute for each of the phrases below.

1. with regard to   _____

2. in the event that   _____

3. subsequent to   _____

4. it is apparent that   _____

5. the possibility exists for _____

28

6. prior to   _____

7. in order to   _____

8. in the neighborhood of   _____

9. at the earliest possible date   _____

10. from time to time   _____

11. in reference to   _____

12. it is necessary that   _____

13. due to the fact that   _____

14. in the amount of   _____

Possible Answers:

1. since	8. about
2. if	9. soon
3. after	10. occasionally
4. obvious	11. about
5. might	12. must
6. before	13. because
7. to	14. for

Exercise:

Eliminate wordiness in the following sentences.

1. Please be advised that the new software has the capacity for analyzing sales figures and budget figures. This program can also compare these figures. The end result will be a report that basically shows the difference between the two.

2. In order to determine your fog index, you should combine together the total number of words divided by the total number of sentences.

3. Due to the fact that Friday is Good Friday, we will close early for the purpose of allowing employees to spend time with their respective families on that day.

4. The consensus of opinion is that the end result will be very favorable.

5. Generally, I would definitely be interested in the given data, but I have really been very busy especially recently.
6. For all intents and purposes, we will basically be applying your payroll deduction toward your union dues.
7. I would like to take this opportunity to thank you in advance for your kind consideration.
8. Even though we have mutually agreed upon the end result, the true facts may still come out.

Possible Rewrites:

1. The new software program analyzes and compares sales and budget figures and produces a report.
2. To determine your fog index, add the number of words and divide by the number of sentences.
3. We will close early on Good Friday to allow employees to spend time with their families.
4. The consensus is a favorable result.
5. Although I've been busy lately, I am interested in the data.
6. We will apply your payroll deduction toward your union dues.
7. Thank you for considering me.
8. Although we've agreed on the result, additional facts may come out.

Now try eliminating clarity and economy problems from a paragraph.

Exercise:

Eliminate unclear wording and wordiness in the following memo.

TO: All Employees
FROM: Keith Edward, Chief Operating Officer

This is to inform you that a new, gray in color Audi was actually left by someone in the back parking lot. Due to the fact that the car has continued to remain there for several weeks and is still yet unclaimed, the company has been given permission by the police to auction off the car if we make a donation of the monies earned to some type of charitable organization. If you are willing and able to be in charge of the auction and to run the subsequent committee, please stop in at this point in time to take the time to discuss the most important and essential elements of the auction proceedings.

Possible Rewrite:

Someone left a gray Audi in the back lot several months ago. Since no one has claimed it, the police gave us permission to auction it off. We'll donate the monies raised to a charity. If you would like to chair the committee that will run the auction, please let me know.

STRAIGHTFORWARDNESS

Straightforwardness refers to the order of words and how close the subject is to the verb. Use S-V-O or subject-verb-object order with strong action verbs. If you write clearly, economically, and in a straightforward manner, your audience will rate your writing high on readability.

Put your words in the right order and use the best grammatical construction to make your point. For example, "We'll *only* write three big papers this semester," suggests we won't do anything else but write these papers. "We'll write *only* three big papers this semester," makes the meaning clearer. Also, try to keep the subject near the verb. Look at the following sentences to see what happens when you don't follow that advice.

Examples

1. In response to your job opening notice concerning the geological technicians' position advertised in the Sunday, October 6, 1998 issue of the *Washington Post*, I am submitting my job application letter.

2. In response to the letter you wrote Dr. Raymond, I am applying for the position of administrative assistant described in the aforementioned letter.

Not only do these sentences have an awkward order, they are unclear as well. Let's consider the following revisions. In the first example, the subject, *job opening notice*, is not near the verb, *submitting*, making this sentence confusing. The following revision seems more straightforward:

1. I am submitting this application in response to your advertisement in the *Washington Post* for a geological technician.

In the second example, it is unclear who wrote the aforementioned letter. Try the following revision instead:

2. I am applying for the administrative assistant position described in your letter to Dr. Raymond.

Avoid the use of redundancy in your writing to ensure greater readability. When we use redundant phrases, we increase the sentence length and violate the 17-word rule. Research shows that sentences containing up to eight words have a "very easy readability" rating, reaching 90 percent of the audience.

Exercise:

Test your readability by rewriting these redundant words or phrases.

1. consensus of opinion _____

2. contained herein _____

3. submitted a resignation _____

4. provide with information _____

5. take under consideration _____

6. basic fundamentals _____

7. close proximity _____

8. cooperate together _____

9. completely full _____

10. end result _____

11. many in number _____

12. future prospects _____

13. sufficient enough _____

14. other alternative _____

15. new innovation _____

16. past experience _____

17. postpone until later _____

18. true facts   _____

19. mutually agree   _____

20. completely finished   _____

21. each individual   _____

22. recurring habit   _____

23. past memories   _____

24. initial preparation   _____

25. more preferable   _____

26. important essentials   _____

27. personal beliefs   _____

28. various different   _____

29. final outcome   _____

30. free gift   _____

31. future plans   _____

32. continues to remain   _____

Answers:

1. Consensus, by definition, is a compilation of opinion.
2. Contained means herein.
3. Resigned—use the verb.
4. Inform—use the verb.
5. Consider—use the verb.
6. Fundamentals and basics are the same thing.
7. Proximity means close.
8. You can't cooperate with yourself.
9. Full means totally or completely.
10. Result means at the end.
11. Number means many.
12. Prospects refers to the future.

13. Sufficient means enough.
14. Alternative means another choice.
15. Innovation means new.
16. Experience refers to the past.
17. Postpone means put off until later.
18. Facts are statements of truth.
19. Agree assumes mutuality.
20. Finished means completely done.
21. Individual means each person.
22. A habit is recurring behavior.
23. Memories are in the past.
24. Preparation means initial.
25. Preferable means better than another choice.
26. Essential means important.
27. Beliefs are personal.
28. Various means different.
29. An outcome is final.
30. A gift is free.
31. Plan implies the future.
32. Remain means continually.

Avoid Trite Sayings, Cliches, and Jargon

Not only do redundancies reduce readability but the use of cliches or trite sayings causes confusion and, even worse, boredom. Most readers skip over cliches in favor of something more substantive. Avoid cliches, but do define each term you use, particularly if you work in a field that uses jargon or technical language a layperson might misinterpret.

Here are the first few paragraphs of a cover letter I received from an individual seeking a writer's position.

My resume, though brief and my little brochure pretty well tell my story. In a nutshell, I tired of the corporate rat race after over a quarter century and for seven years have been my own man.

But as any freelancer knows, things blow hot and cold, and I am certainly not booked to full capacity. A steady thing for a couple of days a week just might be right down my alley.

The writer used at least seven cliches in the first few paragraphs. Cliches are worn-out expressions. Most people skip over them. Be a wordsmith. Don't use tired metaphors or overused expressions.

When your writing loses originality, it also loses persuasiveness. According to Theodore Bernstein in *The Careful Writer*, you don't have to banish all cliches. Use them with discrimination, but eliminate them when they are substitutes for precise thinking.

Avoid trite sayings like: enclosed please find; please do not hesitate to ask; take under advisement; it has come to my attention; maximum optimization; at this point in time; and thanking you in advance for your kind consideration.

If you work in the printing business, you use terms like *blueline* and *dummy* and *mechanical*. Others who work in your industry may understand you, but the average person will not. Beware the use of jargon.

According to the Communication Workshop in Port Washington, NY and the *Secretary's Letter*, we should avoid phrases and cliches like: to be perfectly honest; needless to say; enclosed herewith, please find; if you should have any further questions, please do not hesitate to call; for your perusal, review, and consideration; we deem it advisable; it has come to my attention; the undersigned; pursuant to your request; transparent to the user; and under separate cover.

Avoid Negative Writing

The quickest way to turn off a reader with your writing is to use negative words. Research shows that it takes the mind longer to understand a negative statement than to grasp the same idea expressed in a positive way. Many times writers give unnecessary negative information, like in this cover letter:

ICI Americas is eliminating much of its corporate staff, including myself.

Why not get the interview first before you deliver the bad news? A cover letter is a persuasive document; the purpose is to persuade the reader to review the attached resume.

Instead of providing unnecessary negative information, omit it. When you must provide necessary negative information, do so in the most positive way. Sometimes giving a reason for the negative information softens the message. (See Chapter Nine for more on negative news writing.)

Avoid Passive Writing

According to William Zinsser in *Writing Well*, the difference between active voice and passive voice is the difference between life and death for a writer. In the active voice, the subject performs the action: "The president signed the proposal" versus "The proposal was signed by the president." To avoid writing passively, don't overuse the verbs *to be* or *to have*. When you start a sentence with *there is* or *there are*, you will most likely write passively.

The active voice focuses attention on the doer, while the passive voice features what has been done. If you write actively, you will provide forceful, interesting reading. Most active verbs convey conviction and responsibility. Passive verbs hide the person responsible for the action. Sometimes you want to hide the responsible party. "An increase in union dues is recommended by year end," may work better than, "The union demands an increase in dues by year end" in some cases.

Writers find it difficult to eliminate *to be* and to write actively. Try writing your memo or report first, then edit it to remove the passive voice. The easiest way to change passive to active voice is to put the subject first, closely followed by the verb. "I pledged allegiance to the flag" sounds and reads much better than "Allegiance to the flag was pledged by me." (See Chapter Eight for more on active voice.)

Avoid Stacking

Whenever you stack two or three adjectives in front of a noun, or several nouns in a row, you'll confuse the reader and use unnecessary words. Why say *the very pretty lady* when you could say *beautiful* or *stunning*? Why say *the very unattractive dog* when you could use *ugly*?

Don't worry about withholding information from the reader. Readers don't need to know the machinery was ruggedized, militarized, and field accessible. They only need to know that the machinery works in combat. Keep it simple. Readers will love you for it.

Avoid Italics and ALL CAPS

Research shows that the use of both italics and all capital letters (i.e., CAPS) makes it 20 percent harder for the reader to understand your message. Use italics for titles of literature, foreign words (e.g., *nom de plume*), or emphasis. Don't use it to "look pretty." You'll slow the reader down.

Using all capitals causes another problem. WHEN YOU WRITE IN ALL CAPS, IT'S AS IF YOU ARE SHOUTING AT READERS, AND THEY DON'T LIKE IT!! Fabrik Communications published an E-mail etiquette guide that suggests that messages written in all capital letters are hard to read and users will interpret them as shouting on-line.

When you use acronyms and all caps together, the result can be quite confusing. A memo from personnel read:

BRING YOUR EARS DOWN TO HUMAN RESOURCES TO CORRECT THESE PROBLEMS.

Readability Tips

- Clarity—one meaning
- Economy—17 words
- Straightforwardness—proper order
- Avoid cliches and jargon
- Avoid negative writing
- Avoid passive writing
- Avoid noun and adjective stacks
- Avoid italics and all caps

EARS was an acronym for Employee Action Requests; however, in a memo written in all capital letters, we can't distinguish the meaning.

Avoid the "Me" Attitude

As we discussed in Chapter One, readers don't want to know why the job is perfect for you, the writer; they want to know what you might offer them. The use of the "me" attitude reduces readability because readers perceive no benefit for them.

Exercise: Readability Quiz

Now that we've looked at the many characteristics of readability, let's examine the following samples. Rate the samples using a scale from 1 to 10, with 1 representing the most readable document. Also note the readability problems, using the following criteria: clarity, economy, straightforwardness, and use of cliches, negative writing, passive voice, noun and adjective stacks, italics, all caps, and "me" attitude.

1. Readability score___ Readability problems_____

Gentlemen/Ladies:

Although I would seem to be enormously overqualified for your writer position, I invite you to consider the possibility of utilizing my services.

I'm a Brown University and Penn Law graduate and early retiree from the corporate world where I was a marketing and corporate supervisor for thirty years. I also spent several years freelancing for prestigious companies like Sears, Monsanto, and Quaker Oats.

I must be treated as an outside consultant rather than an employee. At your service if this matter is worth discussing.

Cordially,

Jenna Hillman

2. Readability score___ Readability problems_____

Dear Sir:

I am writing to request that you do not hire me as a part-time writer. Instead, use me as a consultant. By doing so, you will receive a better product and save money.

My company is eliminating much of its corporate staff, including myself. As a result, I must work as a consultant. I would like to show you my portfolio and discuss this opportunity.

Sincerely,

David Henry

3. Readability score___ Readability problems_____

Dear Insurance Carrier:

Amy as you know looks great. She has full range of motion, only mild intermittent discomfort over the wound with deep palpation and heavy activity, and no swelling or significant reactivity. We're going to maintain her on light duty for another two weeks and as of 12/31 bring her up to full duty status. Thanks for letting me participate in the care of your patient.

Sincerely,

Dr. Hal Volpe

4. Readability score___ Readability problems_____

ADDENDUM 1

Should the Township or Municipality where the subject property is located require a certificate of occupancy or other inspection as a condition of occupancy, the Seller agrees to provide that occupancy certificate to Buyer at settlement and Seller further agrees to make any and all repairs as may be required by the Township or Municipality. The parties further understand that an AS IS sale does not release the parties from compliance with a township or municipal ordinance per se.

5. Readability score___ Readability problems_____

Non-Disturbance and Attornment Agreement

1. So long as no default exists, nor any event has occurred, which has continued to exist for such period of time (after notice, if any, required by the Lease) as would entitle the Landlord to terminate the Lease or would cause, without any further action of such Landlord, the termination of the Lease or would entitle such Landlord to dispossess Tenant thereunder, the Lease shall not be terminated, nor shall the Tenant's use, possession or enjoyment be

interfered with, nor shall the leasehold estate granted by the Lease be affected in any other manner, in any foreclosure or any action or proceeding instituted under or in connection with the Mortgage or in case the Mortgagee takes possession of the Real Property pursuant to any provisions of the Mortgage, unless such Landlord would have had such right pursuant to the Lease.

Answers:

1. Readability score 2 or 3. Readability problem: "me" emphasis.
2. Readability score 3 or 4. Readability problems: "me" attitude, negative writing.
3. Readability score 8 or 9. Readability problems: Clarity— What is wrong with Amy and how would a layperson understand this? Although this memo is economical, it is unclear at best.
4. Readability score 7 or 8. Readability problems: economy, passive voice and clarity.
5. Readability score 9 or 10. Readability problems: economy, clarity, italics, passive voice.

Possible Rewrite of Sample 3:

Dear Insurance Carrier:

Amy Taylor, an employee of Pepperidge Farms, has shown great medical improvement. She suffered an accident on the assembly line on 9/14/99 and severely strained her back. After therapy sessions at our office, she now has full range of motion and no swelling or significant reactivity.

We're going to send her back to work as of 12/31/99 on a part-time basis and bring her up to full duty status soon after. Thanks for letting me participate in Amy's care; please contact my office with any questions.

Sincerely,

Dr. Hal Volpe

This letter increases the clarity of the communication by identifying the patient and her injury for the reader. It also provides more detail, leading to greater understanding. It describes the injury in a way that a layperson could understand, thereby increasing its readability score.

Now that you know the many ways to make your writing more readable, consult the following checklist to ensure that you write to express, not to impress your reader.

Checklist: The Power of Words to Express

- Write clearly, with one meaning.
- Use economy; try to keep sentences under 17 words in length.
- Use straightforwardness, keeping subjects near the verbs.
- Avoid wordiness and redundancy.
- Avoid trite sayings and cliches.
- Avoid negative writing by featuring the positive.
- Avoid the passive voice by using active verbs.
- Avoid noun and adjective stacks; use one word rather than many for descriptions.
- Avoid using *italics* and ALL CAPS.
- Remember the "you" or reader attitude rather than the "me" or writer mode.

Part II

Working on Structure and Style

Chapter 4

Easy Formats to Guide Your Reader

Structure That Reaches Readers

Many experts suggest ways in which to format internal and external communication. In this chapter, I'd like to offer several easy formats for writers to follow when composing requests, informative letters, persuasive documents, and good news and bad news memos.

In most cases, using these formats will serve you well and provide structure for your reader. When constructing E-mail messages, memos, letters, and reports, make sure you ask for what you need and explain why you need it.

To write copy that will capture your audience's attention, you must carefully craft purpose, content, and tone. Then you must use a structure that helps your reader. Let's look at a few structure techniques.

KEY TECHNIQUE: USE ENTRANCE AND EXIT RAMPS

Use indentation and exit ramps to lure your readers and to keep their attention.

Always indent your paragraphs to draw readers into your copy. Indentation, or an on-ramp, attracts the reader more than flush left type.

Example:

On-ramp (indentation)

xxxxxxxxxxxxxxxxxxxxxxxxxxxxxxxxxxxxxxxxxxxxxxxxxxxx
xxxxxxxxxxxxxxxxxxxxxxxxxxxxxxxxxxxxxxxxxxxxxxxxxxxx
xxxxxxxxxxxxxxxxxxxxxxxxxxxxxxxxxxxxxxxxxxxxxxxxxxxx
xxxxx.

Exit ramp (short paragraph)

Give your reader easy access to and an easy exit from your writing. Make your first paragraph short to provide reading ease for your audience. Allow the reader to "get off" or exit your document early on. If your readers see that they don't have to read 12 lines before exiting, they are more likely to start reading.

KEY TECHNIQUE: TRY SUBJECT LINES AND POSTSCRIPTS

Use subject lines and postscripts as additional inducements for the reader. A carefully crafted subject line reveals the topic of the E-mail message, report, memo, or letter and can motivate the reader to read the first paragraph. Similarly, most people read the postscript first. A postscript can be a helpful device, especially for persuasive documents. Use it to list your most important point. Now, let's try these techniques in a letter.

Traditional Letter Form

Let's start with the basic letter format. Since most students and employees today use their own computers, many also format their own correspondence.

Example:

Judy Lord   *Heading*
699 Knox Road
Ardmore, PA 19077
(610) 259-1241

January 23, 1999   *Date*

Mr. Mack Penrod
Vice President, Sales
ABC Computing
394 Vesper Road
Knoxville, TN 37966

Subject: Microsoft Word 8.0   *Subject Line*

Dear Mr. Penrod: *Salutation*

Please send me the most current edition of Microsoft Word, which I believe would be the 8.0 version. Would you please send me any appropriate documentation as well? I work at home as a consultant and prepare brochures and newsletters for my clients.   *Body*

As I need your product immediately, please send it in the quickest way, perhaps overnight mail. I have always used your software products and appreciate your quick response. Thank you for handling this request.

Sincerely yours,   *Closing and Signature*

Judy Lord
ALD/jl.245   *Supplement Line*

Attachments (2)   *Attachments*

P.S. I look forward to receiving your software!   *Postscript*

Use a *heading*, including your phone number, even if you're writing from home so that the reader can easily identify you or reach you, if necessary. Include a *dateline* as well. The *inside address* fulfills two purposes: First, you can use the person's title, which most people like to see; second, it routes the letter to the appropriate person even if someone else opens the mail.

The *subject line* clues the reader as to what you might cover in this letter. The *salutation* is also important. Always try to get a name. No one likes unsolicited letters or E-mail messages. If you absolutely cannot find a name, use Dear Student, Dear Customer, Dear Homeowner, or a greeting that identifies the category of person you're writing to. Only use "Dear Sir or Madam" or "To Whom It May Concern" as a last resort. Never use "Gentlemen" unless you know no woman may read the letter. After the salutation, use a colon (e.g., Dear Dean Jordan:). Use a comma after the salutation for personal friends.

Remember to use a short first paragraph to intrigue the reader, and to indent each paragraph for reading ease. Use a *closing* to end your letter: Cordially, Sincerely, Sincerely yours, Regards, Respectfully submitted, etc.

The *supplement line* usually benefits you, the writer, by indicating who formatted the final letter or where you can find this letter on a computer disk. If you plan to enclose a check or another document, indicate how many *attachments* you included (e.g., Attachments: 2). The reader will know to look for the enclosed items.

Also, consider using a *postscript* to catch the reader's attention. If possible, put your main point in the postscript for emphasis or as a teaser.

The Memo or E-Mail Form

Most writers use memos for internal issues and letters for external communication. Sometimes the content suggests whether to use a letter, memo, or E-mail message. In general, continue to use memos internally and letters externally.

In many organizations, E-mail has taken the place of memos because of its speed and ease of use. However, many students and employees misuse E-mail by sending private messages and by forgetting that others may judge their writing skills by viewing sloppy E-mail messages.

Let's review the basic memo format.

Sample:

TO: All Employees   𝒥ℛ
FROM: Johanna Rage, Human Resources Manager
DATE: March 1, 1998
SUBJECT: Holiday policy

Because our employee committee suggested a more flexible holiday policy, we have adopted several options. You may now choose either Columbus Day or President's Day as a paid holiday.

48

Previously, you could select one of these days as a floating holiday; now you may select one as a paid holiday and another day as a floating holiday.

If you have questions about the policy changes, call Alan at 4356.

c: Board of Directors

p.s. Enjoy your extra holiday!!

Use a standard memo format with the following headings: TO, FROM, DATE, and RE or SUBJECT. Use a colon after each capitalized heading and double space the headings. Remember to initial the memo indicating that you've read it and that it contains what you want it to say. Check grammar, spelling, and content before you initial the FROM heading.

Prior to the demise of the carbon copy, the term *cc* was used at the end of a memo to indicate those who would receive carbon copies. Since the carbon copy is extinct, most writers now use *c*, meaning copy.

Copy a person's boss, particularly if your memo cites the person's achievements or accomplishments. When employees receive that kind of recognition, they tend to work harder. Managers often copy employees on their memos on a For Your Information (FYI) basis.

Consider using a postscript in your E-mail message or memo. It catches readers' attention, causing them to look at the subject line. Thus, you can lure readers into your memo in several ways.

TIPS FOR WRITING EFFECTIVE MEMOS

Remember purpose, content, and tone when you write memos. Most memos provide information, describe action, summarize meetings, or make an important point quickly. The purpose does not include a detailed discussion of anything.

For content, stick to one page and start with the bottom line. Get to the point quickly—you only have one page.

For tone, write in the second person. Use "you" as much as possible to establish a personal connection between you and your reader. Once you form this connection with your readers, let's look at some tips to maintain their concentration by improving our memo and E-mail etiquette.

E-Mail Etiquette, or Minding Your Electronic Manners

According to a consumer demand study conducted by the Strategis Group in 1997, U.S. Internet-user households sent or received nine E-mail messages per week. This survey of home use determined that residential users spent six hours per week on the Internet.

According to Marjorie Brody, president of Brody Communications Ltd., a particular form of etiquette applies to E-mail. She suggests seven tips:

1. Watch your words; be concise, eliminating follow-up phone calls.
2. Don't "flame" people or use antagonizing or critical comments.
3. Few people like "spam," or unsolicited E-mail messages.
4. Nothing is private. What will happen if the message is read by someone other than the intended recipient?
5. Keep attachments to a minimum. Most readers hate to download long documents.
6. Consider copying others using the FYI (or For Your Information) designation.
7. Never assume anything. Many users aren't familiar with the lingo and emoticons (:-) for writer is smiling or :-(for writer is frowning that you may know.

According to Barbara Pachter, a communications trainer, sending sloppy E-mail messages is bad business manners. She suggests eight guidelines:

1. Don't contribute to E-mail overload.
2. Keep your message short (one screen or 25 lines).
3. Use short paragraphs.
4. Use a subject line.
5. Don't use all capital letters.
6. Limit each message to one subject area or purpose.

7. Proofread each message.

8. Remember that E-mail is not private.

TIPS FOR WRITING AT CHIP SPEED

Our high-tech, high-speed business world demands to-the-point writing that gets its message across with no wasted words. According to Jack Gillespie, editor of *communication briefings*, even when faxing, sending E-mail, or surfing the Net, we still need to use good writing techniques: simple sentences; short sentences (17 words); "you" attitude toward readers; active verbs; avoiding verbs that masquerade as nouns like consideration (consider) or description (describe); clarity; and short paragraphs with subheads to help your readers.

Now that we know the basic letter and E-mail message formats and how to write at chip speed, let's look at five possible letter or memo formats.

Five Helpful Formats

I. DIRECT REQUEST LETTER OR E-MAIL

When writing a direct request, the most important piece of information to include is why you need the requested item or service and how you will use it. Your reader will usually welcome a direct request. The reader's attitude is positive; she wants to hear from you. Try this format:

Paragraph One	State the request for information or services.
Paragraph Two	State why you need the information and how you will use it.
Paragraph Three	State the specific action for the reader to take.
Paragraph Four	List reader benefits and use a goodwill ending.

If you write to a software company asking to purchase a program, the most important information you can give the company is why you need the software and how you'll use it.

1. Start by requesting the software package.
2. Explain that you'll use it for desktop publishing. Then the company can send you appropriate literature and recommend other software programs.
3. Tell the reader exactly what you want her to do (e.g., send the package by overnight mail).
4. Close with a benefit to the reader like, "I plan to purchase additional software in the near future."

Exercise:

Write a direct request letter asking Ross University for information on its graduate program in public relations. You need more communication skills to advance in your current job as a publications editor. You'd like to start next fall. Use letter format.

Heading:

_____

_____

_____

Date:

_____

Inside Address:

_____

_____

_____

_____

Subject line:

_____

Salutation:

_____

Body:

_____

_____

_____

_____

_____

_____

Closing and signature:

_____

Supplement line:

_____

Attachments:

_____

Postscript:

_____

Remember to explain why you want the graduate information and how it will help you in your current job.

Suggested Answer:

Your letter should look something like this:

Heading

July 1, 1998   *Date*

Lois Poole   *Inside Address*
Graduate Admissions
Ross University
Niles, MI 43215

Subject: Graduate public relations program   *Subject Line*

Dear Ms. Poole: *Salutation*

Please send me information on your graduate program in public relations. I saw your Web page on the Internet.   *Body*

I currently work as a publications coordinator for a large public utility. In my job, I must deal with both employees and customers. A degree in public relations would enhance my ability to advance in the company and to pursue other outside opportunities.

Please send me your catalog and other appropriate information soon as I plan to enroll in the fall. I look forward to becoming a graduate of Ross University's program.

Sincerely,   *Closing and Signature*

Jessica Moffett

JM/1.4   *Supplement Line*

P.S. Please send me the university newsletter as well!   *Postscript*

In the first paragraph Jessica asks for the desired information. The reader at Ross University should welcome this request from a prospective student. Jessica goes on to describe why she needs the graduate information. She describes how she needs this degree to advance in her current job or to look elsewhere. She also explains her current position and in the postscript requests a copy of the university newsletter. Lois Poole now knows what to send to Jessica. She doesn't have to send a generic graduate catalog; she can send specific information.

Jessica closes her letter by including a reader benefit: She may enroll in the fall. She also asks specifically for an action: She needs the information soon so she can register for the fall. Jessica has included the most important elements of a direct request letter; she will most likely receive an appropriate response.

2. INFORMATIVE LETTER OR MEMO

Many times we write to provide information about upcoming meetings, policies, or projects. Usually readers hold a neutral attitude toward informative letters, so the most important goal of this letter is to capture their attention.

Paragraph One   Capture the attention of your audience.
Paragraph Two   Provide the necessary information.
Paragraph Three Present any negative factors; show reasons for these factors.
Paragraph Four   List reader benefits.
Paragraph Five   Provide a goodwill ending.

Capture your reader's attention and then give the required information. If negative factors exist, embed them between other, more positive paragraphs. For example, if a university creates a smoking lounge, a negative factor could be limited times in which smokers could use the room. Never start or end with negatives! Always try to list benefits to the reader and use a goodwill ending.

Exercise:

Write a memo to faculty announcing the appointment of a new department head in engineering. Use Informative Memo format.

TO:

_____

FROM:

_____

RE:

_____

DATE:

_____

BODY:

_____

_____

_____

_____

_____

_____

_____

_____

_____

_____

Suggested Answer:

Your memo might look like this:

TO:	All faculty and staff
FROM:	President Templeton
RE:	New appointment
DATE:	December 11, 1998

I am pleased to announce the appointment of Dr. Melody Henniger as department head of electrical engineering. She comes to us from Fairfield University where she taught for ten years after working for Microsoft, Inc. for twenty years. Dr. Henniger will join us next fall.

Dr. Henniger, a Fulbright scholar, will provide leadership for our electrical engineers and will bring prestige to the university with her national reputation.

Please help me welcome her by attending a reception in her honor next week in the faculty club. She will meet with appropriate faculty members and discuss strategic plans for the fall, when she plans to join us.

Thank you for your help in selecting Dr. Henniger. I look forward to seeing you at the reception to thank you in person.

In the first paragraph, we capture the reader's attention by announcing that a prestigious person will join our staff. We then go on to explain something about Dr. Henniger. We soften the negative factor that she won't join us until fall by stating it in positive terms, and then go on to emphasize that she will bring a national reputation to the university. Finally, we provide a goodwill ending, thanking faculty members for their help and encouraging them to attend a reception.

3. PERSUASIVE LETTER OR MEMO (READER MAY INITIALLY DISAGREE WITH REQUEST.)

Now, let's look at an audience more difficult to persuade. Use these elements of a persuasive document to convince your reader to act for you.

Paragraph One	Catch the reader's interest; establish mutual goals or common ground.
Paragraph Two	Define the problem that will be solved if the request is approved.
Paragraph Three	Explain the solution; show how any negatives are outweighed by advantages of the solution.
Paragraph Four	List all reader benefits.
Paragraph Five	State the specific action you want the reader to take.

Even if the reader disagrees with you, try to establish mutual goals, agree on some point, or establish common ground. Adult learners like to solve problems; give your readers a problem with multiple solutions. Most readers like choices; the multiple solutions allow readers the opportunity to select the option they prefer.

If you must list any negative information, make sure the advantages of the solution outweigh the negative factors. List any benefits that accrue to the reader as a result of the solution to the problem. Most importantly, state the specific action you want the reader to take. Many times readers feel persuaded by the message, but don't know what to do next.

Exercise:

Write a persuasive memo to campus student groups asking them to participate in a "Run for Life" to benefit a local AIDS foundation.

TO: Campus Student Groups
FROM: Student Government Association
RE: "Run for Life" to benefit AIDS foundation
DATE: October 28, 1998
Body
c: Dean of Students

Suggested Answer:

The body of your memo should look something like this:

One of every 10 college students will die from AIDS by the year 2010. We need your help to promote and participate in a run to help these dying students receive the best treatment possible.

Most of us know a friend or acquaintance who has died from AIDS. Let's band together to help students who are suffering with AIDS now and to promote research to find a cure for this horrible disease.

Join us on October 28 by sending participants (runners) or helpers to coordinate this special event.

We will promote your student group by putting your logo on the run T-shirts as well as including you in our news releases sent to on- and off-campus media.

Please call Student Government President Lindsey McHugh at 4267 by September 15 to schedule your runners and helpers.
p.s. Join us to fight a killer of college students.

First, we capture the attention of the students by using a startling and scary fact: College students die from a deadly disease. We then explain how this run can provide a partial solution to a horrible problem. In this case, no negative factors are included in the solution. We go on to list reader benefits—advertising, publicity, and the goodwill of others. We close with a specific call to action for the reader—contact the Student Government President by a deadline. We have indicated to readers exactly what they should do.

Another type of persuasive letter is the cover letter. Some consider a cover letter a combination of a direct request and a persuasive letter. When you write a cover letter for a resume, keep the following tips in mind.

Cover Letter Writing Tips

- List your qualifications in order of relevance to the position, from most to least.
- Make sure to suggest a benefit to the employer, not you, in the first paragraph.
- Quantify your experience whenever possible.
- Begin sentences with action verbs.
- Be concise.
- Omit needless items, especially negative information (for example, "I have little experience in your industry").
- List your technical knowledge (particularly for a resume) early on and in detail, because some resumes are scanned for key words.
- Consider a chart listing the position requirements on one side and your strengths and accomplishments next to the appropriate requirement.
- Proofread. Nothing turns off a prospective employer like a misspelling of her name or the company name or careless typos.
- Don't sell yourself short. This is your opportunity to convey your strengths and abilities and to sell yourself.
- Use an action close like, "I'll call you soon to check on your interviewing schedule."

Remember, an employer wants to receive solicited cover letters; however, your submission may reside in a stack of 100 others.

4. GOOD NEWS LETTER OR MEMO (READER'S ATTITUDE IS POSITIVE.)

Now, let's look at a letter the reader definitely wants to receive. These elements of a good news letter will help you provide structure in an important communication.

Paragraph One   Deliver the good news.

Paragraph Two   Provide any details.

Paragraph Three   Discuss any negative elements.

Paragraph Four   List the reader benefits and close with a goodwill ending.

Take advantage of the opportunity to applaud a colleague or an employee by sending many good news memos. Research shows that employees perform better when they feel appreciated and recognized. In this memo, present the good news and any details of that news. Couch negative elements in between the good news and benefits. List reader benefits to reinforce the news, and close with a goodwill ending.

Exercise:

Write a letter to McDonald's expressing your appreciation for an exemplary employee. You go to the drive-thru window often and the female employee there always serves you well.

Heading

Date

Inside address

Subject line

Salutation

Body

Closing and signature

Attachments

Postscript

Suggested Answer:

Here's how your letter might read:

Maureen P. Steege
275 Bishops Road
Newtown Square, PA 19087
(610) 224-6789

January 5, 1998

Mr. Scott Hipple, Manager
McDonald's Restaurants
478 Parkway
Dallas, TX 99706

Subject: Terrific employee

Dear Mr. Hipple:

I order from your drive-thru window often and enjoy being served by your employee, Miriam Bristol. Regardless of when I use the drive-thru window, she's always in a good mood and seems happy to serve me.

Although I don't eat many fast foods, I come to your drive-thru window for a drink or a frozen yogurt because of the service I receive from Miriam.

Please let Miriam know that her service doesn't go unnoticed. Thanks for looking out for your customers.

Sincerely,

Maureen P. Steege

P.S. Keep up the good work!!

5. NEGATIVE MESSAGE LETTER OR MEMO (READER'S ATTITUDE IS UNFAVORABLE.)

This is the most difficult letter to write—one with a negative message. Use these suggestions to make the bad news easier to bear.

Paragraph One   Establish goodwill.

Paragraph Two   Present the negative message; present reasons for the message.

Paragraph Three Explain positive aspects and reestablish goodwill.

This letter or memo most likely will inspire dread in you and your reader. Establish common ground or goodwill initially. Then give the negative message with the reasons, if possible. To close, explain any positive aspects and reestablish goodwill with your reader.

Exercise:

Write a letter to Decor International and ask them to replace your six white mushroom chairs. The paint on all six chairs is flaking off and you are dissatisfied.

Heading

Date

Inside address

Subject line

Salutation

Body

Closing and signature

Suggested Answer:

Nadia Carlson
133 Paree Drive
Stoystown, PA 15563

July 1, 1998

Decor International
7 Oakmont Place
Pittsburgh, PA 17085

Dear David:

Thank you for sending the furniture we ordered. **[Establish goodwill.]** In the past, we've enjoyed dealing with your company and its products. However, I spoke to you on the telephone yesterday regarding the condition of the six white mushroom chairs I purchased on June 24th.

[Negative message] I've enclosed two photographs of the chairs that illustrate the problem with the paint. You can see it is flaking off in many areas. It appears that the white paint was applied over a finish and does not adhere properly.

Please replace these chairs. If you cannot guarantee the white finish, I will accept the natural finish as a substitute. **[Reestablish goodwill.]** I know you care about customer satisfaction and I look forward to having this problem resolved.

Sincerely yours,

Nadia Carlson

Although no one wants to receive negative news, research shows that we prefer to know the reasons behind the bad news. While most of us have received rejection letters, we feel less devastated when employers list the reasons for the rejection. Sometimes employers don't send letters at all or they send a form letter that reeks of rejection. As a writer, put yourself in the reader's place and write in an empathetic manner.

To design easy formats to guide your writing, use the following checklist.

Checklist: Easy Formats to Guide Your Writing

- Structure your writing to reach your reader.
- Use entrance and exit ramps.
- Try subject lines and postscripts.
- Follow traditional letter or memo formats.
- Watch your purpose, content, and tone in structuring memos.
- Mind your electronic manners.
- Use tips for writing at chip speed.
- Follow the five easy formats for direct request, informative, persuasive, good news, and negative news letters.

Chapter 5

The Power of Visuals, White Space, and Headings

Many writers forget that readers can be put off by an entire page of text with no breaks. In order to appeal to your reader, make use of visuals, white space, and headings. Visuals especially can attract a reader's attention to the text. Most of us are attracted to color and appealing visuals and we look at them before reading. Using the front page of *USA Today* as an example, most people's eyes go immediately to the visual on the bottom left to see what "sound bite" of information the editors present.

Most writers also ignore the power of white space to attract and maintain reader interest. Using white space well includes employing entrance and exit ramps to ease readers into your document and let them know it won't be difficult to read. Use headings whenever possible to break up the text and to allow readers to choose which sections to look at.

Let's look at when to use visuals.

When to Use Visuals

Visuals: When to Use Them

To support text
To convey information
To direct action

Visuals can *support text* by clarifying a confusing or complicated point or by reinforcing a concept. For example, if you're quoting many percentages that could confuse your reader, use a pie chart to illustrate them simply.

Visuals can powerfully *convey information* that is difficult to read in text. For example, tables allow readers to view many pieces of information at one time rather than arduously reading text that describes each number and its meaning.

You can direct action with a visual, referring the reader to a diagram or flow chart that illustrates a process or explains how to follow a set of instructions.

USE VISUALS TO ATTRACT ATTENTION

According to Michael Keene, author of *Effective Professional Writing*, using three visual guidelines can help attract reader attention: accessibility, appropriateness, and accuracy. First, make sure you locate your visual near the text that describes it, providing reader access. Identify the visual, use a short explanation, and frame it with white space. Readers find paging through a report to find a chart annoying. Make sure that the reader can easily find and read your chart or graph and at the same time refer to the related text.

Second, use a visual that is appropriate for its purpose. For example, all the information from a table would not fit in a pie chart. Similarly, many people misuse bar charts by trying to compare ten items at a time, which confuses the audience. Sometimes using a visual might not serve your purpose at all.

Last, ensure accuracy in visuals. Make sure you check your tables for accuracy or your graphs for exact numbers. Did you summarize the important content of the visual in the text and did you acknowledge the source of the data used?

If you follow the guidelines of accessibility, appropriateness, and accuracy, you'll make life easier for your readers.

NEW WAYS TO USE OLD STATISTICS

You have many choices as a writer as to what visuals to use. Let's look at the options.

Tables. Use a table when you need to convey a significant amount of data. Tables are easy to produce and to read.

Visuals: Types

- Tables
- Graphs
  - Bar graphs
  - Line graphs
  - Pie graphs
  - Pictographs
- Structural visuals
- Representational visuals

Writing out and describing every number contained in a table would take many more pages of text. Make sure you follow the accessibility, appropriateness, and accuracy guidelines when designing a table.

The table in Figure 5-1 would rate approximately 5 on a scale of 1 to 10. Can you guess why? How could you improve this table? Did you notice that the numbers don't add up? "Workshops" is actually a category under "Conferences" and the $5,000/$7,000 for "Workshops" are part of the $15,000/$18,000 for "Conferences." You can see how glancing at this table could confuse rather than assist your reader.

Figure 5-1.

Wallace University Research Budget Requests
($ thousands)

Category	*1998 Actual*	*1999 Projections*
Travel	40	45
Paper presentation	12	15
Conferences/	15	18
Workshops	5	7
Visiting lecturers	30	35
Laboratories	43	48
Released time	220	230
Total	**360**	**391**

Graphs. As writers, we can select what kind of graph to use as a visual. Most authors select bar graphs to show comparisons among several items, for example, nuclear arms in the U.S. versus Iraq. Bar graphs or horizontal bars usually compare quantitative information (See Figure 5-2). Figure 5-3 displays effective use of a stacked bar graph allowing for easy comparison of data. Figure 5-4 displays the appropriate versus inappropriate use of picturing trend data.

Figure 5-2a. Bar graph and line graph using same data

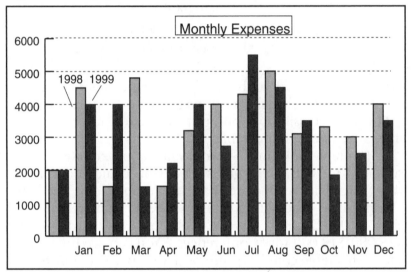

Figure 5-2b. The simple bar graph and line graph do not add data, but display two variables side by side, allowing for easy comparison.

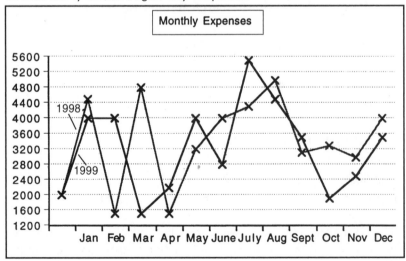

Figure 5-3a. Stacked bar graph and stacked area graph using same data

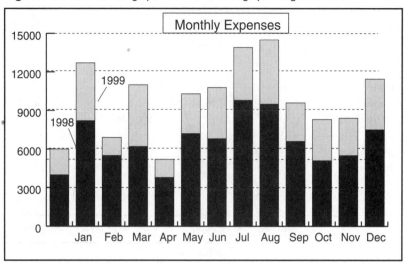

Figure 5-3b. Example of a stacked bar graph and stacked area graph that add data from one year to the next, representing two years' total expenses

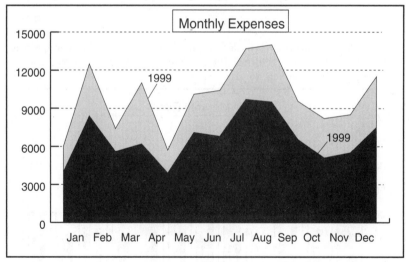

Figure 5-4a. Visualizing a trend over multiple years

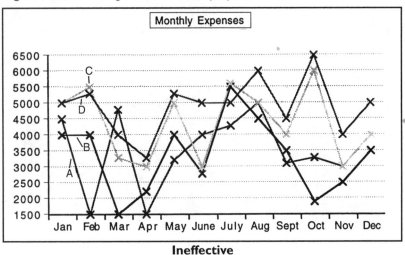

Ineffective

Figure 5-4b. The line graph is ineffective because it shows similar data trends that are hard to distinguish in this format. The standard bar graph is more effective for comparing this data from year to year.

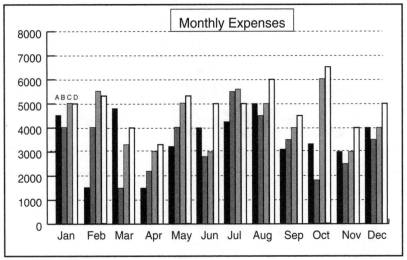

Effective

Exercise:

Create a bar graph comparing the number of students at private universities (1.4 million) versus the number of students at public universities (2.2 million).

Line graphs are primarily used to indicate precise changes over time, so you might use a line graph to show chronological information such as the history of the stock market and its stability. Refer to Figure 5-4. Pie graphs show percentages of a whole and should not be used to convey complex information. Pie graphs also show the relationship of parts to a whole. Figure 5-5 shows how data can be illustrated effectively in a pie graph when the same data would be ineffectively presented in a bar graph. Figure 5-6 shows how a bar graph can be effective when there is too much information to be conveyed in a pie graph.

Exercise:

Create a line graph of the enrollment at Wallace University from 1985-1995. Use these statistics: 1985-4500, 1986-4555, 1987-5540, 1988-5120, 1989-5430, 1990-5560, 1991-5600, 1992-4980, 1993-5450, 1994-5570, 1995-5760.

Exercise:

Create a pie graph of the first-year students, sophomores, juniors, and seniors at Wallace University assuming the following numbers: first-year students—1575, sophomores—1400, juniors—1400, seniors—1385.

Recently, in part due to the influence of *USA Today*, pictograms or pictographs have become popular. These graphs use simple images or icons to represent quantities similar to a bar graph or to show a few important statistics in picture form. For example, you might compare consumption of white wine versus red wine in America by drawing two bottles and filling one bottle more than the other to show greater consumption.

The only disadvantage of pictographs is accuracy. It would be difficult to exactly measure 1.1 million gallons versus 2.3 million gallons on a picture of two bottles. Figures 5-7 and 5-8 depict pictographs of World Wide Web sites visited by home users and major league baseball teams with the best winning percentages in opening day games, respectively.

Figure 5-5a. A pie graph is an effective way to show percentages. The whole pie equals 100% and each slice represents the percentage allocated to that slice.

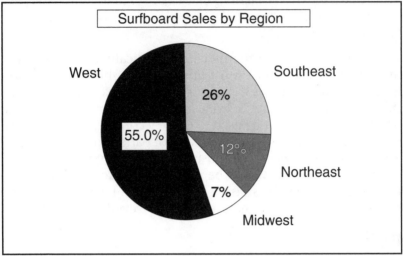

Effective

Figure 5-5b. The same data in bar graph form does not effectively demonstrate that the selected items are parts of a whole equaling 100%.

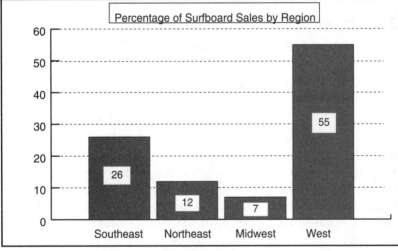

Ineffective

Figure 5-6a. This bar graph is an appropriate way to compare data over time and determine trends.

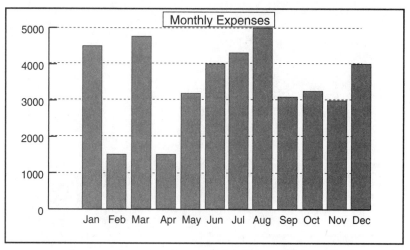

Figure 5-6b. This is the same data in pie graph form. Notice that the data are not easy to read and the trend over time is not clear.

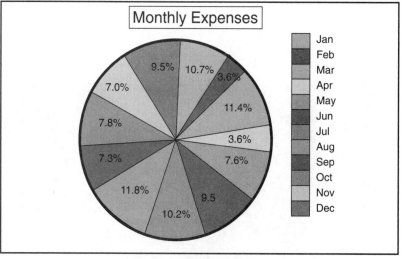

Ineffective

Figure 5-7.

The right start

Major league baseball's 1998 regular season opens today. Teams with the best winning percentages in opening day games:

Mets, 23-13 .639

Mariners, 13-8 .619

Yankees, 56-40 .583

Giants, 55-41 .573

Orioles, 54-42 .563

Figure 5-8.

In sites

World Wide Web sites home computer users most say they visited in a typical month in 1997:

aol.com 46%
yahoo.com 38%
netscape.com 31%
miscrosoft.com 22%
geocities.com 21%
excite.com 20%

Exercise:

Create a pictograph using the following statistics: Compare the number of au pairs and nannies (1 million) in the United States versus stay-at-home moms (2 million).

Structural Visuals. Structural visuals are diagrams, flow charts, or organization charts that detail a complicated process. In sets of instructions you can often find structural visuals to help you load a camera with film or follow a scientific process. Structural visuals help readers to picture complex patterns. The example of an organization chart in Figure 5-9 details the reporting relationships for a company that offers services for senior citizens. Remember that sometimes employees report directly to a supervisor and sometimes there is an indirect or dotted-line relationship.

Figure 5-9.

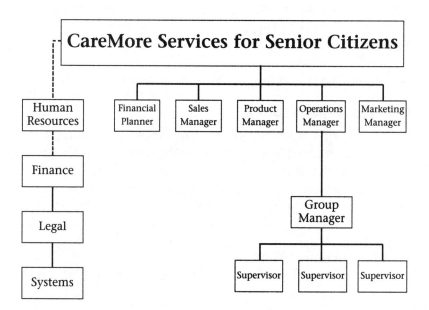

Exercise:

Create an organization chart for a club, work situation, or organization you belong to. Make sure to show reporting relationships.

Representational Visuals. Simply put, representational visuals are pictures or photographs that enhance text and grab reader attention. Many major newspapers today use color photographs to attract reader attention and sell newspapers. The old adage, "A picture is worth a thousand words," applies here. If you use a powerful photo, words may not be necessary.

Exercise:

For each of the following topics, list the type of visual aid that would best support the main message.

A. How snakes adjust to seasonal changes
B. Small talk and the art of mingling
C. Why cigarette vending machines must be outlawed
D. Why to invest in the U.S. stock market today
E. How to juggle
F. The Siberian tiger
G. The most successful marketing campaigns of Pepsi Cola

Possible Answers:

A. Pictures of snakes before and after they shed their skin
B. A bulleted chart with five successful opening lines for meeting someone
C. A graph of total vending machine sales of tobacco products
D. A line graph of NASDAQ performance over the last ten years
E. A line drawing or flow chart of the steps to learn simple juggling
F. A photograph of tigers
G. Pictograms of Pepsi's financial success through ad campaigns

How can you adapt visuals for specific audiences? Placement of a visual at the end of a document indicates lack of importance. Placing a visual prior to the text tells the readers that the visual is more important than the text. Many experts suggest placing the visual immediately after the text for effectiveness. Don't underestimate the power of visuals to gain and maintain reader interest!

Prevent Eyestrain with White Space

The use of ample margins draws readers' attention to the center of the page. Indented paragraphs provide relief from eyestrain. Use white space between paragraphs to make each one look like an easy-to-read unit. Long blocks of copy look gray and difficult to tackle. Like visuals, use white space to appeal to readers, tempting them to read on.

Remember to use entrance and exit ramps as white space. Consider leaving a border of white space around your text for reader ease.

Use Headings to Structure Your Writing

Most companies and organizations maintain a style guide that will point you in the right direction regarding the use of headings. If your professor or company does not use a style manual, try these suggestions: Use headings to help readers find specific parts of a report; to present your outline and organization to readers; to ensure your own organization; or to announce new topics.

Remember to make headings grammatically parallel; put ideas of similar content and function into similar form. The headings may appear together in a table of contents, like this:

Writing for Business
Writing for the Reader
Preparing Your Text

or

Business Writing
Writing for the Reader
Prepare Your Text.

The first example is grammatically parallel or similar; the second one is not.

Grammatically parallel:

The Overall View
The Terminal Phase
The Constant Bearing Concept

Not grammatically parallel:

The Overall View
About the Terminal Phase
To Understand the Constant Bearing Concept

Use a heading every two or three pages; use no more than seven minor headings per major heading. Try the following levels of headings.

Four Levels of Headings

A level	MAJOR HEADING (centered, all caps)
B level	Minor Heading (centered)
C level	Subheading (flush left)
D level	Paragraph Headings (indented)

Exercise:

Add headings to the following block of text. Don't get carried away. Remember the guidelines.

Put clarity in your writing.

The most valued writers in the organization write honestly. They transfer information so their audiences know it and feel it as they do. Granted, there are times you may want to be vague to leave room for debate and creativity. But much writing on the job is vague, undisciplined and imprecise.

One of the problems that plagues writing on the job is "third-degree writing"—writing that's too general and doesn't honestly represent what's in the writer's mind. Example: The boss sends a memo saying that the situation in the office is getting serious.

Situation isn't what the boss means. It's a third-degree word. Imagine a ladder, often called the ladder of abstraction in writing. The ladder has three steps. The bottom rung represents third-degree writing—situation in the office. The next rung is second-degree writing—dispute. The top rung represents first-degree writing—employee disagreement about smoking on the job.

The boss actually wanted to talk about the dispute employees are having over smoking on the job. But the boss called it a situation. The boss is a third-degree writer. First degree—disagreement about smoking, second degree—dispute, and third degree—situation.

If you want to convey a message, use concrete words. Avoid office equipment when you mean computers and writing implement when you mean pen. If you want people to understand you, be as specific as possible. Dr. Walter St. John thinks that vague wording just about guarantees confusion. He writes about it in *The Handbook of Basic Managerial Communication* for the Friendly Ice Cream Corporation. He says that well-intentioned managers who try to be democratic or non-directive often offer statements like "Joe, give this a top priority" or "Jill, I need this out as soon as possible." To avoid misunderstandings, specifically state when you need the job done.*

*Reprinted with permission from *communication briefings*, "Power-Packed Writing That Works."

Possible Rewrite:

PUT CLARITY IN YOUR WRITING

The most valued writers in the organization write honestly. They transfer information so their audiences know it and feel it as they do. Granted, there are times you may want to be vague to leave room for debate and creativity. But much writing on the job is vague, undisciplined, and imprecise.

Third-Degree Writing

One of the problems that plagues writing on the job is "third-degree writing"—writing that's too general and doesn't honestly represent what's in the writer's mind. Example: The boss sends a memo saying that the situation in the office is getting serious. *Situation* isn't what the boss means. It's a third-degree word.

Imagine a ladder, often called the ladder of abstraction in writing. The ladder has three steps. The bottom rung represents third-degree writing: *situation in the office*. The next rung is second-degree writing: *dispute*. The top rung represents first-degree writing: *employee disagreement about smoking on the job*.

The boss actually wanted to talk about the dispute employees are having over smoking on the job, but instead referred to *the situation*. The boss is a third-degree writer.

First degree—disagreement about smoking
Second degree—dispute
Third degree—situation

Specific Words Tell It Like It Is

If you want to convey a message, use concrete words. Avoid using *office equipment* when you mean *computers* and *writing implement* when you mean *pen*. If you want people to understand you, be as specific as possible.

Vague Wording Causes Problems

Dr. Walter St. John thinks that vague wording just about guarantees confusion. He writes about it in *The Handbook of Basic Managerial Communication* for the Friendly Ice Cream Corporation. He says that well-intentioned managers who try to be democratic or non-directive often offer statements like "Joe, give this top priority" or "Jill, I need this out as soon as possible." To avoid misunderstandings, state specifically when you need the job done.

Now let's review the use of visuals, white space, and headings in the following checklist.

Checklist: The Power of Visuals, White Space, and Headings

- Make sure visuals support text, convey information, or direct action.
- Use the visual guidelines of accessibility, appropriateness, and accuracy.
- Learn about all types of visuals and pick the best one for your text.
- Use white space generously for reader comfort.
- Remember to use entrance and exit ramps as white space.
- Use margins as white space.
- Use the headings recommended in whatever style guide your organization uses. (Consider the *Associated Press Style Guide* as a default.)
- Use grammatically parallel headings, at least one for every two or three pages of text.

How to Start and Stop

Gaining Attention

I once gave a lecture at Villanova University about using exciting introductions to attract an audience. One day, a female student took my advice. As she presented her speech, the other students began to fidget and stir uncomfortably in their seats. She had chosen to start by describing how she and her boyfriend had experimented with many illegal drugs.

Several students were embarrassed for her and glared at me as if I should stop her speech. She went on and on, providing intimate details of their drug use. Silence overwhelmed the classroom. Finally she said, "That was the story of Laura Edward, a young lady with a difficult decision to make." The class collectively gasped in relief that she wasn't the one announcing her drug use. She certainly got our attention—a key ingredient to a good introduction.

Most writers suggest starting with a quotation, a story, an anecdote, an example, or even a rhetorical question to attract readers to your document. Once you get their attention, then you can work on keeping it. According to Susan Perloff, a Philadelphia writer and writing teacher, anecdotes add spice and attract attention to your introduction. Anecdotes show rather than tell something about the subject and make great leads because of their memorability.

Use strong introductions and conclusions in your writing. The reader might read only the beginning or the end, so you need to gain attention in both places. Many times readers pressed for time read only an executive summary, an introduction, or a conclusion. For this reason, the introduction and conclusion must provide critical information as well as motivation for the reader to absorb the entire document.

Particularly in a persuasive document, the writer must attract the reader's attention. Suppose you want to propose an on-site fitness center at your company. If you start with low employee morale as a rationale, you might not motivate the reader. But if you researched the topic and found that productivity would increase because of decreased sick days or better health among employees, you might attract management's attention.

To attract an employer to read a resume, a good cover letter is necessary. To attract a reader to the body of a report or letter, a good introduction is necessary. On the flip side, a strong summary may be the only thing a reader remembers, so don't hesitate to repeat the premise or overriding purpose of your piece there. It's important to write attractive introductions and conclusions.

Introductions: CPO Method

Context
Purpose
Organization

Openings That Get to the Point

According to Michael Keene, author of business writing texts, the CPO method of writing introductions works best. Many writers establish a context or common ground with the reader and announce the purpose of the communication, but most writers don't forecast the organization of the letter, report, or other document. Forecasting the organization of a longer letter or report lets the reader know what you will cover and where to find a particular section of interest quickly.

When you listen to a sermon or homily, you'll notice that good speakers often announce that they will cover three key points, thus forecasting the organization of their address. The audience knows when the speaker is on point one, two, or three, and can follow the presentation of the material. Likewise, letting your readers know what's coming shows respect for their time and attention.

According to Melody Templeton, professor at Villanova University, the various goals of introductions include:

- To create a positive relationship with the audience (similar to context).

- To support or complement your message in content, tone, and style (similar to purpose).

- To involve the audience and gain the attention of or "hook" your readers.

Exercise:

Analyze the following two introductions to see if they use the CPO method.

Ten Steps to Improve What You Write

This section offers you 10 easy steps to take to improve what you write. You don't need any special knowledge. What you need: the desire to improve your writing—and persistence.

You can try all the steps at once, or you can work on one each day, each week or even each month.

You can set your own goals, but the steps are so easy you can start trying them today. If you persist, you'll sharpen your prose, boost your productivity and enhance your chances to succeed.*

Context_____

_____

_____

Purpose_____

_____

_____

Organization_____

_____

_____

*Source: *communication briefings*

ANSWERS:

Context: The author sets the tone by letting the reader know how she can write better in ten easy steps.

Purpose: The purpose seems clear—to improve your writing and boost your productivity at the same time.

Organization: The organization is forecast in the first sentence, describing what will occur in this particular section.

How to Put Power and Punch in Your Proposals

You just met with the boss, who seems to like your great new idea for reducing costs and increasing profits. The boss says, "Write it up. Get a proposal to me by Friday."

Many people have had this experience. Unfortunately, many good ideas die at this point, when those with the great ideas fail to clearly, persuasively, and forcefully "write up" the analysis of a problem and recommend how to solve it.*

Context_____

_____

_____

Purpose_____

_____

Organization_____

_____

_____

ANSWERS:

Context: Talking about common experiences creates a context with the reader.

Purpose: The purpose isn't totally clear, but suggests the need for a clear, persuasive write-up.

Organization: This introduction doesn't seem to forecast the organization of the article.

*Source: *communication briefings*

Exercise:

Using the following tips, write a CPO introduction on E-mail etiquette:

1. Watch your words; be concise, eliminating follow-up phone calls.
2. Don't flame people or use antagonizing or critical comments.
3. Few people like "spam," or unsolicited E-mail.
4. Nothing is private. What will happen if the message is read by someone other than the intended recipient?
5. Keep attachments to a minimum. Most readers hate to download long documents.
6. Consider copying others in the office using the For Your Information (FYI) designation.
7. Never assume anything. Many users aren't familiar with the lingo and emoticons that you may know.

_____

_____

_____

_____

_____

_____

Possible Answer:

E-Mail Etiquette

Many of us send E-mail messages, but we may not realize the necessary etiquette we should use. This report will suggest ways to write effective, well-mannered E-mail messages. We will discuss seven tips for constructing E-mail messages.

Exercise:

Write a CPO introduction to a report for high school seniors on the benefits of a college education.

_____

_____

_____

_____

_____

Possible Answer:

We all have to make the choice between working and going on to college. It's important to evaluate the benefits and negatives of each choice. This report will outline the three primary reasons to choose college and the possible negatives of this choice. It will then discuss reasons for working rather than going on to college, and the negatives of this choice.

Exercise:

Create a CPO Introduction for two of the following topics:
How to set up a new aquarium
Opening a bed & breakfast
Financing your first home
Comparison of two good computer systems
The life of Martin Luther King

1. _____
_____
_____

2. _____
_____
_____

Remember, when writing introductions, keep the first few paragraphs short, allowing the reader an exit or "off-ramp"—a way to get out quickly if the document doesn't apply to him. Once you've hooked the reader, you must keep him interested. Transitions can serve as a way to maintain reader interest, because they add coherence to a paragraph and smooth the way for reader understanding.

The best writers use transitions wisely. Some common transitions include:*

Go-ahead words—and, moreover, furthermore, also, for instance

New-idea words—thus, so, and so, therefore, consequently, accordingly

---

*Source: *communication briefings*

Summary words—as a result, at last, finally, in conclusion, in short

Change-idea words—but, yet, nevertheless, otherwise, although, despite, however, conversely

Link-cause-and-effect words—that caused, as a result, that produced, consequently

Referring words—they, these, though, not one, all but two, without exception

Restricting and qualifying words—provided, in case, if, lest, when, occasionally, even if, never

How to End on a Strong Note

Most readers remember best what they read last. Conclusions, therefore, provide a great opportunity to move your reader in the direction you choose. In any conclusion, briefly summarize the entire document. Repeat the major points, for emphasis. Reemphasize the importance of the topic and provide recommendations, if appropriate. A persuasive document often requires recommendations, while an informative letter might not.

Always recommend action of some kind. The most common mistake writers make is to persuade readers and then leave them hanging, with nothing specific to do.

If you used a story, anecdote, or quote to start with, can you bring the story full circle or end with the same example? Many people like closure, so starting and ending with the same story or example completes the process for them. What works best is to start the document with a story that you don't finish until the end of the document, leaving the reader hanging on in suspense.

Exercise:

Can you tell whether the following example from an article on gender communication summarizes, repeats major points, recommends an action, or reemphasizes the importance of the topic?

Gender Specific Communication As a Reflection of Gender-Specific Worldviews*

Differences between female and male styles of interaction arise from the fact that men's and women's worldviews basically differ in several points. The sexes have distinct viewpoints and attitudes towards life, think differently and therefore do not have the same notions of what is essential. As our personality, which includes our views and our thinking, is reflected in our conversations, sex-specific worldviews result in a sex-specific way of communication.

The genders have different opinions about the purpose conversation should serve. Deborah Tannen has characterized those gender-specific worldviews in a way I can support for the most part. According to Deborah Tannen, women approach the world as individuals in a network of interpersonal connections, designed to support each other. The aim of communication is to create and maintain support and confirmation in a conversation. In a conversation women therefore concentrate on whether the speaker remains aloof or tries to get closer.

Men, on the other hand, look upon the world as hierarchically structured where it counts to achieve and maintain a high status, to stand up against other people and to preserve independence. For men, conversations are part of this struggle for a good social position, and so communication serves them as a means to gain and keep the upper hand and to challenge others. In a conversation they rather focus on whether the interlocutor possibly tries to outdo, belittle or patronize them (Tannen, 1992).

Tannen mentions that women are also interested in achieving a high status and want to avoid being defeated, but they do not give it special emphasis; similarly, men want to preserve intimacy and avoid isolation too, but it is less important for them. I share Deborah Tannen's point of view in this matter, but she adds that women tend to pursue such male goals "in the guise of connection" and that men tend to pursue such female goals "in the guise of opposition."

This is possible, but in my opinion Deborah Tannen contradicts herself. If gender-specific styles of conversation exist in the way she describes them, then men and women have no other choice than to make use of their usual interactional style, although they concentrate on aims which are usually the focus of the respective other sex. In my opinion, connection and opposition are not disguises but

*Source: http://www.suska.ch/papers/gender/2.html.

rather methods; why should women and men be able or want to change their way of communication, which is rooted in them and familiar to them, just because they want to achieve something that is not typical of their sex?

To sum it up, it may be said that men's conversational style as a consequence of their outlook on life tends to be competitive, while women, due to their worldview, prefer a cooperative conversational style.

Exercise:

Analyze the last paragraph or summary of the preceding article to ascertain its effectiveness.

Summary of important points?_____

_____

Major points reemphasized?_____

_____

Recommendations made?_____

_____

Actions stated?_____

_____

Suggested Answer:

The concluding paragraph summarizes the intent of the article. Only one major point is mentioned. No clear actions or recommendations appear.

Exercise:

Write a better conclusion to the article on gender communication.

_____

_____

_____

_____

_____

_____

Possible Answer:

Gender-specific communication reflects gender-specific world-views. Each gender has different opinions about the purpose of conversation. According to Deborah Tannen, the purpose of communication for women is to create and maintain relationships and to avoid isolation. Men use conversation as part of the struggle for a good social position, so communication serves as a means to gain and keep the upper hand and to challenge others. To sum up, it may be said that men's conversational style tends to be competitive as a consequence of their outlook on life, while women prefer a cooperative conversational style due to their worldview.

Let's look at another conclusion from an earlier chapter in this book.

The following checklist will help you to speak "right" to the crowd. Follow these simple tips to quickly improve your writing.

1. Find out as much as possible about your reader.
2. Use a "you" attitude.
3. When in doubt, write clearly, for a 12-year-old reader.
4. Motivate a layperson audience to read.
5. Feature a detailed process for an expert.
6. Use the bottom line for an executive audience.
7. Tell user audiences how to do it.
8. For a complex audience (an individual who fits more than one category), combine audience types.
9. For a mixed audience, write to laypeople.
10. Remember, all readers want to know what's in it for them.
11. Overcome the objections of a hostile audience.
12. Use nonsexist language.

Using a list allowed me to summarize key points and to make recommendations at the same time. I called for action by listing ways writers could reach readers. I didn't reemphasize the importance of the topic, so we could rewrite this conclusion.

Exercise:

Read the following short conclusions and determine how you could improve them.

1. Today I've gone over the three main steps you can take to protect your car from theft. Keep them in mind the next time you go to the mall!

Improvements:_____

_____

_____

_____

_____

2. Today we've looked at the reasons for changing our meal plan. First, it will allow student athletes who practice during currently scheduled dining hours to have dinner without added expense. Second, it allows dining service workers to enjoy flexible working hours. Third, the change will eliminate some of the waste we now experience at our university. Please vote yes on changing our meal plan at the student center today!

Improvements:_____

_____

_____

_____

_____

3. Picture yourself free of carrying keys, credit cards, your driver's license, membership cards, even cash. Imagine going out to dinner or to the movies or even taking a vacation without carrying a wallet or purse. That's what our future looks like when the "Eyedentification" program begins. You can be unencumbered!

Improvements:_____

_____

_____

_____

_____

In exercise 1, you could repeat the three main steps in case readers can't remember or didn't read the whole article. In exercise 2, you could state a benefit to the reader or average student who may not be an athlete or work in the dining hall; otherwise the paragraph serves as a good conclusion. In exercise 3, repeat the definition or main points of the Eyedentification program to help the reader.

Now that you can critique and write effective introductions and conclusions, use this checklist to review your new techniques:

Checklist: How to Start and Stop

- Use Context-Purpose-Organization introductions.
- Attract readers with a story, anecdote, question, example, or startling statistic.
- Maintain reader interest by using transitions.
- Conclude by summarizing, repeating main points, making recommendations, and suggesting an appropriate action.

Chapter 7

Brush Up on Your Grammar

When many of us hear the word *grammar* we cringe, thinking back to sixth grade English when we were forced to stand in front of the class and conjugate irregular verbs. For others, *grammar* connotes those picky points we don't need to worry about. But the use of correct grammar can make or break you professionally.

Professors, colleagues, and customers expect you to use language correctly and not make errors that educated people avoid. Recently, in an interview for a management position, a candidate misused many words. Although he seemed qualified, his resume and presentation skills suggested that he didn't recognize the importance of grammar and the correct use of language to his advancement. He didn't get the job.

In this chapter we'll review some basics we all forget. We'll discuss some common errors and problems and possible solutions that can increase our credibility in the workplace.

Common Problems and Solutions

ABSTRACT WRITING

As we discussed in earlier chapters, use picture words or specific words, not vague words like *situation* or *document*.

Abstract: There is an important *document* on my desk that might interest you.

Ideas for some grammar problems are from "The 76 Most Common Grammar Errors and How to Avoid Them," *communication briefings*.

Concrete: Your *annual review* is on my desk; it might interest you.

Note the difference between *document* and *annual review.*

AGREEMENT

Every verb must agree in number with its subject. If the subject is singular, use a singular verb; if the subject is plural, use a plural verb. Also, don't mistake the object of a prepositional phrase for the subject of the sentence and choose the wrong number (singular or plural) for the corresponding pronoun or verb.

Examples:

Each of the executives wants his or her own office.

The secretary and the treasurer are responsible for presenting the annual report.

Every file drawer was searched.

Exercise:

In the following examples, indicate whether agreement is used correctly. If not, fix the offending parts of speech.

1. The corporation published their annual report.

   _____

2. Every employee must report to their supervisor.

   _____

3. Neither the secretary nor the typist has received her check.

   _____

4. There's two versions of the report.

   _____

5. The best part of the seminar is the speeches.

   _____

6. Somebody in the audience lost their purse.

   _____

7. Neither the manager nor her administrative assistant wants her hours changed.

_____

8. The committee made their final recommendation.

_____

Possible Answers:

1. **Incorrect**—Corporation is singular. The sentence should read "its annual report."
2. **Incorrect**—The sentence should read "his or her supervisor."
3. **Correct**
4. **Incorrect**—There's is a contraction of there is, which is singular. The sentence should read, "There are two versions of the report."
5. **Correct**
6. **Incorrect**—The sentence should read "her purse."
7. **Correct**
8. **Incorrect**—Committee is singular. The sentence should read "its final recommendation."

APOSTROPHE

The apostrophe usually shows possession or marks omissions in contractions. A notable exception is *it's*. *It's* is a contraction of *it is*. No apostrophe is needed to show possession, as in *its effectiveness*.

BECAUSE VERSUS *AS*

Avoid using *as* instead of *because*.

Incorrect example:
We had a day off *as* it was Good Friday.
Correct example:
We had a day off **because** it was Good Friday.

COMMAS

Most business writers get carried away and add commas every so often to spice up their copy. Use commas to indicate short pauses. The best way to tell whether you need a comma is to read a sentence aloud to see if you pause.

Some other simple rules follow:

- Don't separate a subject from its verb. Example: "The actor, sighed."
- Use commas to set off words or phrases that are parenthetical (meaning they are not integral to the sentence). Example: "The river, which was muddy, flowed by the downtown area."
- Current journalistic style calls for eliminating the last comma in a series of items. Other style manuals call for including it. Choose the style you wish and use it consistently.

Exercise:

Add appropriate commas.

1. We'd like to process this form for you but you'll have to notarize it.
2. One package was lost and two were damaged but the rest arrived safely.
3. No one even his best friend knows where Ben goes during lunch.
4. The format of a training session usually includes a trainer introducing the program going over the goals and objectives and using several methods of teaching.
5. He invited Faith Billy Chrissy and Steven to the birthday party.

Answers:

1. We'd like to process this form for you, but you'll have to notarize it.
2. One package was lost and two were damaged, but the rest arrived safely.
3. No one, even his best friend, knows where Ben goes during lunch.

4. The format of a training session usually includes a trainer introducing the program, going over the goals and objectives and using several methods of teaching.
5. He invited Faith, Billy, Chrissy and Steven to the birthday party.

COMMONLY MISUSED WORDS

Exercise:

Try to identify the differences between these like-sounding or similar words. If you find one set particularly difficult, make a note of it on your computer or somewhere you'll glance at it frequently to check yourself.

accept, except
affect, effect
all ready, already
among, between
amount, number
assure, ensure, insure
bad, badly
center around, center about
cite, site, sight
complement, compliment
continual, continuous
credible, creditable
eminent, imminent
fewer, less
good, well
imply, infer
it's, its
principle, principal
there, their, they're
whose, who's
your, you're

Answers:

accept, except: *Accept* means to receive; *except* means to omit.

affect, effect: *Affect* is a verb meaning to influence; *effect* can be a noun meaning a result or a verb meaning to bring about.

all ready, already: *All ready* means that everyone or everything is ready; *already* means previously.

among, between: Use *between* with two persons or things; use *among* with more than two.

amount, number: *Amount* refers to a sum or a quantity not able to be counted; *number* refers to a quantity able to be counted.

assure, ensure, insure: *Assure* means to give confidence; *ensure* means to make certain; *insure* means to indemnify or safeguard.

bad, badly: *Bad,* an adjective, should not be confused with *badly*, an adverb.

center around, center about: Avoid using either of these incorrect terms; use *center on.*

cite, site, sight: *Cite* means to mention as proof; *site* is an area; *sight* is a sense.

complement, compliment: *Complement* completes; *compliment* is an expression of praise.

continual, continuous: *Continual* means repeated often; *continuous* means without interruption.

credible, creditable: *Credible* means believable; *creditable* means deserving esteem.

eminent, imminent: *Eminent* means distinguished in a profession; *imminent* means threateningly near at hand.

fewer, less: *Fewer* refers to countable objects; *less* refers to uncountable quantity.

good, well: *Good* is an adjective; *well* is usually an adverb.

imply, infer: *Imply* means to suggest; *infer* means to conclude.

it's, its: *It's* is a contraction of *it is*; *its* is the possessive form.

principle, principal: *Principle* means law or truth; *principal* means main (as an adjective) or leader (as a noun).

there, their, they're: *There* is an adverb indicating location; *their* is a possessive pronoun; *they're* is a contraction of *they are*.

whose, who's: *Whose* is the possessive form of the pronoun *who*; *who's* is a contraction of *who is*.

your, you're: *Your* is the possessive form of the pronoun *you*; *you're* is a contraction of *you are*.

DOUBLE NEGATIVES

Avoid the confusion of double negatives.

Incorrect example:

We won't attend the affair on June 4 nor even the one on June 5.

Use *or* because *won't* covers both dates.

EXCLAMATION POINTS

Don't overuse them or they become like cliches—boring!!!!

FORMER

Be careful when you use this word.

Incorrect example:

He was a former president.

Isn't he still a former president? Change it to:

He was formerly president.

GUNNING-MUELLER FOG INDEX

Use the index to make sure you write at a level your reader will find comfortable. See Chapter One to calculate your fog index.

HYPHENS

Many people confuse hyphens and dashes. Dashes are used like commas; hyphens join two or more words that express a single concept when those words precede a noun.

Exercise:

Decide whether or not to use a hyphen in the following examples.

1. face to face
2. hand in hand
3. face to face communication
4. down to business professor
5. side by side interaction

Answers:

1. face to face (doesn't modify anything)
2. hand in hand (doesn't modify anything)
3. face-to-face communication (modifies the noun)
4. down-to-business professor (modifies the noun)
5. side-by-side interaction (modifies the noun)

IRREGARDLESS

Avoid this word; most experts consider it substandard. Use regardless.

ITALICS

Remember to use italics sparingly because we read italic type 20 percent more slowly than regular type.

JARGON

You can impress those who understand you with your technical language, but you will confuse an audience that is unfamiliar with technical terms.

LATIN USAGE

Don't confuse *e.g.* with *i.e. Exempla gratia* means *for example* and is used to exemplify a point. **Example:** Select other subjects, e.g., philosophy, astronomy, and computer science. *Id est* means *that is* and is used to explain a point. **Example:** Send the package to the bursar, i.e., the person who collects all the money.

LINKING VERBS

Some verbs like *appear, feel, look, seem, smell, sound,* and *taste* can function as linking verbs. When they do, adjectives, not adverbs, should follow them. **Example:** He felt bad (not badly) about hitting Brett.

MISPLACED MODIFIERS

Place modifiers (words or phrases that limit or qualify) as close as possible to the word or words they describe. Place the following adverbs after the verb, not before: *almost, even, hardly, just, merely,* and *only.*

Incorrect example:

I only have two dollars. (This implies you own nothing else in the world.)

Correct example:

I have only two dollars.

Incorrect example:

I almost read half the book.

Correct example:

I read almost half the book.

NONSTANDARD LANGUAGE

Check your dictionary to avoid using unacceptable words like *ain't, copacetic, irregardless,* or *hisself.*

NUMBER STYLE

Spell out numbers from zero to ten and all numbers that begin sentences.

Incorrect example:

1989 was an exceptional year.

If you don't want to write out the date, say, "In 1989."
Use digits for numbers greater than ten and for ages. Watch for trouble with dollar signs, as in *$5 million dollars.* Because we've already used the dollar sign, we've just indicated *five million dollars dollars.*

PARALLEL CONSTRUCTION

Use parallel structure for sentence elements joined by coordinating conjunctions (*but, and, or, nor, for*). Also use parallel structure in headings and subheadings.

Incorrect example:

A student can learn typing, filing, and to write.

Correct example:

A student can learn typing, filing, and writing.

PRONOUN USE

Learn the three cases of pronouns so you don't mix them up in your writing.

Subjective pronouns:

I, you, he, she, it, we, they, who

Objective pronouns:

me, you, him, her, it, them, whom

Possessive pronouns:

my (mine), your (yours), his, her (hers), its, our (ours), their (theirs), whose

Never use *myself, yourself,* or *themselves* as the subject or object of a sentence.

Incorrect example:

The authorities met with the managers and myself.

Use *me* instead of *myself.*

PUNCTUATION

We've already discussed apostrophes, commas, hyphens, and exclamation points. Let's look at the use of **semicolons**. Use semicolons sparingly in business writing. Whenever possible, turn a semicolon into a period and use two separate sentences.

Use a semicolon to separate two closely related independent clauses not joined by a coordinating conjunction like *and* or *but.*

Example:

Be careful to turn off the printer; don't try to change the toner cartridge while the machine is still on.

Periods specify a full stop, while semicolons signal a shorter stop. Use periods to end complete sentences; use semicolons to separate closely related clauses.

Use a **colon** after an independent clause to introduce a list, an example, or an explanation. Also use colons after the salutation of a business letter, between the hour and minutes of time, and between a title and a subtitle.

Example:

We did not open an account with First Union for two reasons: They don't offer interest-bearing checking and their advertising is misleading.

Use a **dash** much like a comma—to pause or to set off a thought that is loosely connected to the sentence. Like commas, do not overuse dashes.

Parentheses are used to enclose material that is even more loosely connected to the sentence. Parentheses minimize the element that is set off. You may enclose one or more complete sentences within parentheses.

Use **quotation marks** to enclose titles of short works like articles or speeches or to enclose words taken from special vocabularies or used in a special sense. Use quotation marks to enclose quotes short enough to work into your own text (three lines or fewer). If you quote a passage longer than three lines, set it off by indenting it on all four sides. Put commas and periods inside closing quotation marks; put semicolons and colons outside. Question marks and exclamation points should be put inside the closing quotation marks only when they are part of the matter being quoted.

Use **ellipsis points** sparingly. Remember those three dots that mean *and so on*?

Example:

Please bring with you several outfits for rainy weather, several pairs of shoes or boots, several pairs of woolen socks, several protective hats...

Exercise:

Add to or correct the punctuation in the following sentences.

1. The telephone call brought the news they had been waiting for their design won top honors.

2. Esther Henry the companys oldest employee walks to work every day.

3. Every class is faced with the same problem high absenteeism.

4. You may want to rewrite the section of your paper that begins The Problems with Spinning in Politics.

5. Your Weston stock you won't believe this just jumped 4 points.

6. The three most important points are 1) the time schedule 2) the cost 3) and who will perform the work.

7. The new manager he is a close friend of Eric's will start work on Monday.

8. The meeting on February 5 lasted for three hours therefore, please allow three hours for the next visit.

9. Your report seems interesting, and you wrote it well.

10. Ken left for Singapore on April 16 1998 and never came back.

Answers:

1. The telephone call brought the news they had been waiting for—their design won top honors. (Use a dash or a colon.)

2. Esther Henry, the company's oldest employee, walks to work every day. (Use commas to set off the parenthetical or noncritical phrase; use an apostrophe to show possession.)

3. Every class is faced with the same problem: high absenteeism. (Use a colon or dash.)

4. You may want to rewrite the section of your paper that begins, "The Problems with Spinning in Politics." (Use a comma and quotation marks. Note the period inside the close quotation mark.)

5. Your Weston stock, you won't believe this, just jumped 4 points. (Use commas or dashes.)

6. The three most important points are: 1) the time schedule; 2) the cost; and 3) who will perform the work. (Use a colon before the list and semicolons or commas to separate the items within the list.)

7. The new manager (he is a close friend of Eric's) will start work on Monday. (Use parentheses because this portion of the sentence is not necessary; the sentence makes sense without it.)

8. The meeting on February 5 lasted for three hours; therefore, please allow three hours for the next visit. (Use a semicolon before *therefore*.)

9. Your report seems interesting and you wrote it well. (Remove the comma; it separates two connected thoughts.)

10. Ken left for Singapore on April 16, 1998, and never came back. (Add commas after the day and year.)

REDUNDANCY

Avoid redundant words and phrases.

Exercise:

In the following examples, remove the redundant term.

1. revert back   _____

2. bitter tasting   _____

3. 8:45 p.m. at night   _____

4. somewhere in the neighborhood of   _____

5. completely full   _____

6. end result   _____

7. true facts   _____

8. future prospects   _____

Answers:
revert, bitter, 8:45 p.m., about, full, result, facts, prospects

SPELLING
To avoid spelling problems, read prolifically. When you learn to recognize words, you'll spell more accurately. Proofread your work and keep a dictionary close by; don't rely entirely on a computer spellchecker. You may have particular words that stump you. Try your hand at these exercises.

Exercise:
Find the misspelled word in each group and correct it.

1. liquefy   _____
   disappear   _____
   swirling   _____
   dissolve   _____
   no error   _____

2. inexorable   _____
   mercyful   _____
   potable   _____
   arboreal   _____
   no error   _____

3. unnecessary   _____
   carnage   _____
   wierd   _____
   judgment   _____
   no error   _____

4. roses   _____
   goverment   _____
   absence   _____
   churches   _____
   no error   _____

5. primarily _____
   principal _____
   principle _____
   receit _____
   no error _____

6. erred _____
   millionaire _____
   misanthrope _____
   lieutenent _____
   no error _____

7. adjournament _____
   caucus _____
   contagious _____
   digestible _____
   no error _____

8. aquired _____
   brief _____
   contemptible _____
   height _____
   no error _____

9. benefited _____
   appealed _____
   refered _____
   equipped _____
   no error _____

10. biased _____
    aberation _____
    wholly _____
    vacuum _____
    no error _____

Answers:

1. No error
2. merciful
3. weird
4. government
5. receipt
6. lieutenant
7. adjournment
8. acquired
9. referred
10. aberration

Exercise:

Pick the correct spelling of each word.

1. a. municipal
   b. municiple
2. a. committment
   b. commitment
3. a. privilige
   b. privilege
4. a. memento
   b. momento
5. a. exceed
   b. excede
6. a. allotted
   b. alotted
7. a. separate
   b. seperate
8. a. accommodate
   b. accomodate
9. a. liaison
   b. liason
10. a. occasion
    b. occassion

11. a. occurrance
    b. occurrence
12. a. erroneous
    b. erronous

Answers:

1. a
2. b
3. b
4. a
5. a
6. a
7. a
8. a
9. a
10. a
11. b
12. a

THAT VERSUS *WHICH*

Use *that* when the words following it are necessary to identify the word *that* refers to. Use *which* when the words following it are not necessary to identify the word it refers to. When using *which*, use commas to separate the clause. When using *that*, don't use commas.

Example:

The park that I drive through provides great scenery.

Example:

The park, which I drive through each day, provides great scenery.

TYPEFACE

Avoid using extensive italic type. Use italic and boldface sparingly for special emphasis. Use serif type for body copy and san serif type for headlines. Styles such as Courier have serifs, the small finish strokes on each letter. Sans serif type styles, which don't have the finish strokes, are harder to read.

VERBS

Remember how to conjugate verbs so you use the correct tense. Most regular verbs form their past tense and past participle by adding *-d* or *-ed*. These irregular verbs cause us more trouble:

Verb	Past Tense	Past Participle
begin	began	begun
choose	chose	chosen
raise	raised	raised
speak	spoke	spoken
bring	brought	brought

WHO VERSUS WHOM

Use *whom* when the word serves as an object and *who* when it serves as a subject.

Examples:

Who won the prize?

The new manager, *who* moved here from Frackville, called a meeting.

Whom did you pay?

With *whom* were you working?

YOU AND I

Many writers confuse *you* and *I. Between you and I, we have the knowledge* should read, *Between you and me, we have the knowledge.*

Grammar Tips and Traps

Let's look at some grammar problems that can alienate your reader. The English language contains many irregular verbs, but that is no excuse for using an improper form. Readers expect good use of the language from writers. In fact, as writers, we use words as our tools to get the job done. The less we know about the tools, the fewer options we have for using them.

TIP: Avoid the use of *to be* and *to have*.

TRAP: Relying on a computer spellchecker; keep a dictionary nearby instead.

TIP: Use active verbs to aid readability.
TRAP: Using cliches frequently.

TIP: Know the difference between *i.e.* and **e.g.**
TRAP: Calling a corporation or a company *they* instead of *it*.

TIP: Make sure each verb agrees in number with its subject.
TRAP: Starting a sentence with *there is* or *there are*.

TIP: Use the words *lay* and *lie* correctly: *Lie down if you don't feel well*, but *Lay the book on the table.*
TRAP: Switching from one verb tense to another unnecessarily.

TIP: Make sure your sentence contains a verb and its subject.
TRAP: Punctuating phrases as sentences.

TIP: Watch for run-on sentences.
TRAP: Using *it's* as a possessive.

TIP: Use parallel structure in headings and subheadings.
TRAP: Using the term *centers around*. A center is a point.

TIP: Memorize the spelling of irregular plurals like *alumni* and *analyses*.
TRAP: Using *amount* when you mean *number*.

TIP: Use *businessperson* rather than *businessman*.
TRAP: Confusing *who* and *whom*.

TIP: Proofread everything you write, preferably after you put it aside for awhile.
TRAP: Misusing *I* and *me*. Use *me* after a preposition and *I* after comparisons.

TIP: Watch your use of collective nouns; generally treat them as singular.
TRAP: Overusing commas.

TIP: Use parentheses sparingly.
TRAP: Using the word *irregardless*.

TIP: Use periods for a full stop and semicolons for a shorter stop.
TRAP: Using redundant words and phrases.

TIP: Use apostrophes to show possession.
TRAP: Using double negatives.

TIP:	Use the Gunning-Mueller Fog Index to write at an appropriate level.
TRAP:	Overusing exclamation points.
TIP:	Remember to use italics sparingly.
TRAP:	Mistaking hyphens for dashes.
TIP:	Spell out numbers from zero to ten and all numbers that begin sentences.
TRAP:	Trying to impress readers with technical jargon.
TIP:	Whenever possible, turn a semicolon into a period and use two separate sentences.
TRAP:	Forgetting to use a colon after an independent clause to introduce a list.
TIP:	Use a dash much like a comma, to pause or to set off a thought that is loosely connected to the sentence.
TRAP:	Using ellipsis points regularly.
TIP:	Double check everything for personal grammar errors.
TRAP:	Assuming the reader knows everything you do.

Grammar plays a major role as a tool that structures our language. Mastering proper grammar shows respect for readers and will enhance their opinions of us as writers. Use the following checklist to brush up on your grammar skills.

Checklist: Brush Up on Your Grammar

- Avoid abstract writing by using picture or specific words.
- Make sure verbs agree in number with their subjects.
- Use apostrophes to show possession or mark omissions.
- Watch your use of *because* and *as.*
- Don't get carried away with comma use.
- Be careful with like-sounding or similar words like *affect* and *effect.*
- Don't overuse exclamation points!!!
- Be careful when using the word *former.*
- Use the Gunning-Mueller Fog index to write at a level your reader understands.
- Don't confuse hyphens and dashes.
- Never use the substandard word *irregardless.*
- Use italics sparingly.
- Avoid the use of jargon.
- Watch the meaning of common Latin terms.
- Watch the use of linking verbs.
- Place modifiers as close as possible to the word they modify.
- Check your dictionary to avoid using nonstandard language.
- Spell out numbers from zero to ten and numbers that begin sentences.
- Use parallel construction for sentence elements joined by conjunctions.
- Learn the three cases of pronouns.
- Make sure you understand punctuation and how to use it.
- Avoid the use of redundant words and phrases.
- Read often to avoid spelling problems.
- Use serif type for body copy and sans serif type for headlines.
- Review the conjugation of irregular verbs.
- Use *whom* when the word serves as an object and *who* when it serves as a subject.
- Don't confuse the use of *me* and *I.*

Chapter 8

Using Action Verbs

Readers can tire easily and often find passive writing boring. Those of you who are old enough to remember the primers with Dick and Jane know they exemplify active writing. (If you don't remember, ask your parents!) *See Dick run. See Jane run. See Spot run after Dick and Jane.* Although these sentences seem overly simple, you can easily identify the subject, verb, and object.

On the other hand, phrases like, *It was stated in the report, It has been determined that, A report was sent to all divisions by the manager,* and other passive constructions are more difficult to read and bore the reader. Researchers recommend that only 10 percent of your writing use the passive voice. Use active writing whenever possible. In order to write actively, avoid the use of the verbs *to have* and *to be.* Starting a sentence with *There is* or *There are* will generally guarantee use of passive writing. Make your writing come alive with Subject-Verb-Object construction.

Active Writing Motivates Readers

Recall the discussion on economy from Chapter Three that suggested avoiding the passive voice. Writing passively takes more words and often produces cumbersome sentences. For example, "It was stated by the provost that," takes longer to say than the active version, "The provost stated." Active writing, on the other hand, motivates readers by providing forceful, interesting reading.

In some cases, when you want to be vague or when speaking of certain crimes, you might want to use the passive voice: "She was raped." If the thing being done is more important than the doer of the action, use the passive voice. "The store opened at 10 a.m." works better than "Grant opened the store at 10 a.m." because who opened the shop is less important than when it opened. If you want to soften a thought, you might consider using the passive voice. Instead of, "Send me a check today," you might write, "I'd appreciate receiving your check soon." In general, though, try to eliminate use of the passive voice.

Exercise:

Replace the passive voice with active voice.

1. On July 9, information was requested by you about our library holdings.

_____

_____

2. It was announced by the vice president that refunds will be given to customers concerned about harmful chemicals in the product.

_____

_____

3. It is expected that we will see you at your next appointment.

_____

4. Your assistance would be appreciated by us.

_____

5. Please be advised that you are requested to call the provost as soon as possible.

_____

6. The report was received by the employees.

_____

7. It was requested by you that we sit together.

_____

8. Fewer incidents were suffered by students last year than ever before.

_____

_____

9. It was stated in the report that our sports programs rival the Big Ten.

_____

_____

10. It is my estimation that you will complete your thesis sometime next year.

_____

_____

Possible Answers:

1. You requested information about our library holdings on July 9.
2. The vice president announced that concerned customers will receive refunds if they fear harmful chemicals in our products.
3. We expect to see you at your next appointment.
4. We would appreciate your assistance.
5. Please call the provost as soon as possible.
6. The employees received the report.
7. You requested that we sit together.
8. Students suffered fewer incidents last year than ever before.
9. The report stated that our sports programs rival the Big Ten.
10. You will complete your thesis sometime next year.

Michael Ivers writes that the active voice focuses attention on the doer while the passive voice focuses on what has been done. Most active verbs carry more power than passive ones. Think of, "I believe in life everlasting" versus "Life everlasting is believed by me."

In the active voice, the doer usually appears before the verb, as in, "I pledge." In the passive voice, the doer appears at the end of the sentence, for example, "Parents are often disrespected by their children." Active language imparts a sense of authority. It shows people taking responsibility for their actions.

Let's try a few more exercises to rid our writing of passive expression.

Exercise:

Eliminate the passive voice, replacing it with active verbs.

1. There are no standard definitions of child abuse that we know of.

_____

_____

2. All of the employees are in need of training to improve their skills.

_____

_____

3. A syllabus will be provided by us to assist each department.

_____

_____

4. Experts were involved in helping us to formulate the guidelines for the syllabus.

_____

_____

5. The kind of behavior that can be disruptive to the team cannot be permitted by managers.

_____

_____

6. It was stated by the lawyer that the victim could not be responsible.

_____

_____

7. There were 21 references to advertising in the text.

_____

_____

8. There is a conflict between the marketing and advertising departments.

_____

_____

9. The student recreation center is requesting the help of the students to allocate monies for new fitness equipment.

_____

_____

10. The Student Trustees are requesting the help of the student body to pass a referendum for Internet access networking.

_____

_____

Possible Answers:

1. We know of no standard definitions of child abuse. (Put the subject first, then the verb.)
2. All employees need training to improve their skills.
3. We will provide a syllabus to assist each department.
4. Experts helped us formulate the guidelines for the syllabus.
5. Managers cannot permit behavior that disrupts the team.
6. The lawyer stated that the victim could not take responsibility.
7. The text referred to advertising 21 times.
8. The marketing and advertising departments face a conflict.
9. The student recreation center requests the help of students to allocate monies for new fitness equipment.
10. The Student Trustees request the help of the student body to pass a referendum for Internet access networking.

Exercise:

Replace passive verbs with active writing.

1. On June 1, information was requested by you about the upcoming Graduate Record Exam.

_____

_____

2. It was announced by the president that raises will be given to all employees complaining about inflation.

3. Please be advised that you are requested to contact this office as soon as possible.

4. It is expected that you will be billed for the flowers next month.

Possible Revisions:

1. On June 1, you requested information about the upcoming Graduate Record Exam.
2. The president announced that employees complaining about inflation will receive raises.
3. Please contact this office as soon as possible.
4. We will bill you for the flowers next month.

Exercise:

Revise the following passage using the active voice.

A report was sent to all offices by the president, who had been asked to make comments on the reorganization. It was stated in the report that fewer layoffs were suffered by employees last year than ever before. Furthermore, the new Chief Operating Officer was named. All questions were to be handled by her. The report was received enthusiastically by the employees.

Possible Revision:

The president sent a report about the reorganization to all offices. The report stated that fewer employees suffered layoffs last year than ever before. The president named a new chief operating officer who will handle any questions. Employees received the report enthusiastically.

Use Subject-Verb-Object Style

To change from passive to active writing, use the subject-verb-object order. Most passive writing uses the object-subject-verb order. When I write a report or letter, I use the verbs that come naturally to mind. Then I revise my writing by eliminating as many *to be* verbs as possible. I also try to purge my writing of the object-subject-verb order. Most people can't write actively without rewriting. It takes a lot of effort!

Exercise:

Try rewriting these sentences using the subject-verb-object order.

1. It is primarily the audience who determines your success.

_____

_____

2. The more you know about the group who will be listening to you, the greater your chances of success.

_____

_____

3. A good audience analysis before your speech is critical.

_____

_____

4. A conservative Republican audience will probably be more opposed to easy availability of abortions than a liberal Democratic group.

_____

_____

5. Many vocal factors are included in how we communicate.

_____

_____

6. Shifting weight from the left to the right foot may not even be noticeable to the speaker, but can make the audience seasick.

_____

_____

7. Here are some hints to combat uncontrollable movements.

_____

_____

8. Be on the lookout for repetitive phrases.

_____

_____

9. These are common fillers for the Generation X age group.

_____

_____

10. There are also phrases which are repeated frequently in different geographic regions.

_____

_____

Possible Answers:

1. The audience primarily determines your success.
   (subject)   **(verb)**   **(object)**
2. The more you know about the group who will listen to you, the greater your chances of success.
3. You should prepare a necessary audience analysis before your speech.
4. A conservative Republican audience will probably oppose the easy availability of abortions more than a liberal Democratic group.
5. We include many vocal factors in our communication.
6. The speaker may not notice that she shifts from the left to the right foot, but the audience may feel seasick.
7. You can use these hints to combat uncontrollable movements.
8. Look out for repetitive phrases.
9. Generation Xers use these common fillers.
10. Speakers from different geographic areas use phrases typical of their regions.

Many times just placing the subject first in the sentence will enable you to write an active S-V-O sentence. Compare the power and economy of the previous S-V-O sentences to the passive, long-winded alternatives.

Many writers weaken their documents when they bury the action in a noun rather than using verbs.

Example:
The advertising director failed to give an explanation of the plan.

Revised:
The advertising director failed to explain the plan.

Example:
It is our expectation that we will see productivity improvement when the technicians learn the new process.

Revised:
We expect the technicians to produce more when they learn the new process.

Example:
The registrar is responsible for the processing of the schedules.

Revised:
The registrar processes the schedules.

Note how much shorter the revised sentences are. Also note that we changed the nouns into verbs to make the sentences active.

According to the authors of *Power-Packed Writing That Works*, we should "purge the putrid passive" from our writing. They assert that using too many passives weakens your prose, makes it dull and hard to read, and adds useless words. According to the authors, passive writing fails to give anyone credit for what occurred.

Example:
To make it easy for mothers of toddlers to participate in the program, a simple sign-up procedure has been created.

Who created the simple sign-up procedure?

Revised:
Early Childhood Development has created a simple sign-up procedure that makes it easy for mothers of toddlers to participate in the program.

Avoid Noun Writing

Using nouns instead of verbs also tremendously weakens your prose. In order to value verbs, scan your writing for other structures that hide verbs. Try using verbs to see how concise and active the phrases become.

Exercise:

Replace the following nouns with verbs.

made a change _____

made an improvement _____

made an acquisition _____

made a decision _____

made a presentation _____

made a recommendation _____

made a suggestion _____

made a choice _____

Possible Answers:

changed, improved, acquired, decided, presented, recommended, suggested, chose

Exercise:

Correct these verb-noun phrases by selecting one verb to replace them.

came to a realization _____

conducted an investigation _____

had an expectation _____

gave authorization _____

took under consideration _____

submitted a resignation _____

reached a conclusion _____

used a quotation _____

Possible Answers:

realized, investigated, expected, authorized, considered, resigned, concluded, quoted

    Active writing using verbs and the S-V-O order can revolutionize the style and effectiveness of your writing. Keep that in mind as you use the following checklist.

Checklist: Using Active Verbs

- In general, avoid using the passive voice.
- Use the passive sparingly, such as when you don't want to take responsibility for an action or when you are referring to a victim.
- Use active verbs, not *to be* or *to have*.
- Use Subject-Verb-Object construction.
- Don't bury the action of your sentence in a noun, for example, *explanation* versus *explained*.
- Remember, the passive voice makes writing dull and cumbersome.

Part III

Situational Writing

Chapter 9

Delivering Bad News

If you want to annoy a reader, use negative words. Not only are negative words annoying, but research shows that it takes the mind longer to understand a negative statement than a positive one. In Chapter Four we talked about delivering bad news in letters or memos. Let's review the format we discussed for presenting negative information.

Negative Message Letter or Memo

(Reader's attitude is unfavorable.)

Paragraph One — Establish goodwill.

Paragraph Two — Present the negative message; present reasons for the message.

Paragraph Three — Explain positive aspects and reestablish goodwill.

The reader won't want to receive the bad news. Establish common ground or goodwill first, then give the negative message, with the reasons if possible. To close, explain any positive aspects and reestablish goodwill with your reader.

Giving a reason for your negative information softens the blow. I once had an interview for a college teaching position. The interview started at 7:00 a.m. and, after eight hours of interviews, I had to give an hour-long lecture. Then the college held a wine and cheese party in my honor. Several people pulled me aside and said I was the best contender for

129

the position and they looked forward to working with me. I left very tired, but satisfied that I had the job.

I waited for the call. After several weeks, I received a standard rejection letter in the mail. No reasons were given. I was upset. I called the contact at the university and inquired why I was not selected. She said that they chose someone with over ten years of teaching experience; I had only three years of experience. If the university had stated the reason in the letter, I wouldn't have felt so rejected. Consider softening the bad news with a reason or rationale.

Sometimes you must not only give negative news, but you must deliver it to a hostile group. The following tips will help you write for them.

How to Present Negative Messages

According to *communication briefings*, a five-part strategy works best when presenting bad news.

- *First*, announce your position and offer basic evidence.
- *Second*, and very importantly, recognize the audience's possible objections. List each possible objection to your position. Disarm the audience by agreeing with them on some points, if possible. Use your research to recognize the audience's position.
- *Third*, refute each audience objection by using your evidence. Use facts or statistics to make your point.
- *Fourth*, argue your position. Amplify each argument here.
- *Fifth*, conclude with a summarizing statement that repeats specific actions you want the audience to take.

How Not to Offend Your Reader

No one likes to receive a past due bill that states, "If you do not remit this payment by May 1, we will send this information to a collection house." Maybe you're waiting for the insurance company to pay you or maybe you really owe the money. Regardless, no one likes to receive insults or threats.

Most negative news is delivered in this harsh fashion. Sometimes readers become so annoyed that they withhold the payment as a punishment. Let's try some exercises to cast negative news in a more positive light.

Exercise:

Revise these sentences to eliminate negative messages.

1. If we don't receive your payment by May 1, you'll be billed an additional fee.

_____

_____

2. Unless you send us this information, we will not process your claim.

_____

_____

3. Until you receive our permission, you may not begin the job.

_____

_____

4. If you sent your resume, as you claim, we did not receive it.

_____

_____

5. Did I miss anything in class yesterday? *(My all-time favorite question—Author)*

_____

_____

6. Due to an error in processing your order, it will be billed more than once to your account. A credit has been issued and we hope you have not been inconvenienced.

_____

_____

7. We regret to inform you that the merchandise you ordered is not available. Because of this, we have been forced to cancel your order.

_____

_____

8. Please don't hesitate to call if you have trouble understanding these instructions.

_____

_____

9. If you took the test, as you claim, we have failed to receive your score.

_____

_____

10. Unless you send us this data, we will not issue your coverage.

_____

_____

11. My experience has been limited to part-time jobs.

_____

_____

Possible Answers:

1. Please send us your payment by May 1 to avoid the late fee.
2. We will process your claim as soon as we receive your information.
3. You may begin the job as soon as you receive our authorization.
4. Please send us your resume; we don't have a record of receiving it.
5. What do I need to know from the lecture yesterday?
6. We apologize for the inconvenience of our processing error. We have corrected your account.
7. We are sorry that your merchandise is unavailable at this time.
8. Please call if you have any questions.
9. Please send us your test score again as we have not received it.
10. We will issue your coverage as soon as we receive your data.
11. My experience includes several part-time jobs.

Exercise:

Write a letter to the dissatisfied customer in the following scenario, presenting negative news to a hostile person.

Scenario: Amy McVay took an expensive dress to the dry cleaner; it had ten buttons down the front. She failed to notice the handwritten sign that stated, "We're not responsible for buttons, zippers, or Velcro." When Amy picked up her dress it no longer had the ten attractive buttons. You work for the cleaner. Write a letter to Amy telling her that you cannot find the buttons. Try to reestablish goodwill.

First paragraph: Establish goodwill.

_____

_____

_____

_____

Second paragraph: Present the negative message and reasons for it.

_____

_____

_____

_____

Third paragraph: Explain positive aspects and reestablish goodwill.

_____

_____

_____

_____

Possible Answer:

Your answer should include an apology and an explanation of why you cannot replace the buttons. You should also provide a free coupon or some way of assuaging Amy's anger. Assure her that you do not normally lose buttons and try to reestablish goodwill.

How to Trigger Positive Responses

Sometimes readers don't need to know all the negative information. For example, in a resume cover letter you might not want to mention that you can't find a job. Does it make you seem marketable? What benefit does the reader or do you achieve from mentioning your current job status? Get the interview first, then discuss your status.

DO: Highlight the positive nature of the bad news.
DON'T: Give unnecessary negative news.

DO: Couch the negative news in the middle of more positive aspects.
DON'T: Reject someone with no reason.

DO: Word your negative news in the most positive way.
DON'T: Put down or talk down to the reader.

Exercise:

Rewrite these sentences with a positive emphasis.

1. Although I haven't worked for months, I have years of experience in data processing.

_____

_____

2. Although the freelance market has dried up in recent years, I am still available for hire.

_____

_____

3. We shall have to institute legal action against you if you do not submit your payment by July 1.

_____

_____

4. Church of the Saviour is eliminating much of its staff, including myself.

_____

_____

5. I am writing to request that you do not hire me as a part-time writer.

_____

_____

6. But as any freelancer knows, things blow hot and cold and I am certainly not booked to full capacity.

_____

_____

7. At your service if this matter is worth discussing.

_____

_____

8. We note in your letter that you claim not to have received your order.

_____

_____

Possible Answers:

1. I have years of experience in the data processing area.
2. I am available to provide freelance work for you.
3. Please submit your payment by July 1 to avoid legal action.
4. (Eliminate this entire sentence.)
5. Consider me for a full-time or part-time job.
6. I am available to serve your organization in a freelance capacity.
7. I look forward to discussing this matter with you.
8. We're sorry you didn't receive your order.

Exercise:

Write a rejection letter to a graduating senior who applies to your company, an insurance firm, for a public relations job. You chose someone else based on on-site psychological testing of applicants.

_____

_____

_____

_____

_____

_____

_____

_____

Possible Answer:

Dear Drew:

Thank you for interviewing with Weaver Insurance. We enjoyed meeting with you and discussing career opportunities.

After reviewing the results of your testing, we concluded that the "fit" here with the rest of our team wasn't perfect. Your results indicate that you are a self-starter and that you are highly analytical. We were looking for a slightly different mix.

We hire for several public relations positions each year and generally these employees move quickly to management levels. We'd like to consider you for the next available position as each department requires a different team composition.

Thank you again for the time you spent with us. We look forward to speaking with you again in the future.

Sincerely,

Grant Crawford
Human Resources Manager

Tips for Handling Customer Complaints

Angry or frustrated customers may write to you demanding action. An article in *communication briefings* notes that in responding to complaints, writers sometimes forget to listen to the actual complaint, or worse yet, they complain back. Often writers defend the organization without sympathizing with the customer, propose vague solutions, or confuse the customer with technical jargon.

Complainers want satisfaction in terms of recognition of their problem and correction by the organization. They desire empathy with their plight. These effective response techniques will guide you:

1. Recite the facts; repeat them back to the customer.

2. Empathize with the customer. Customers need to know you feel the same way they do.

3. Put the problem at a distance. Make sure the customer knows the problem is an exception.

4. Cite a specific action you will take to correct the problem.

5. Reestablish goodwill. Offering a gift or coupon often works well.

In summary, when writing negative news, try to start and end with goodwill. Don't feel you must share every negative aspect with your reader. Try to give reasons for any negative information. Use the following checklist for help.

Checklist: Delivering Bad News

- Share reasons for the bad news.
- Learn techniques for addressing a hostile audience.
- Highlight the positive nature of the bad news.
- Don't give unnecessary negative news.
- Couch the negative news in the middle of more positive aspects.
- Word your negative news in the most positive way.
- Don't belittle or talk down to the reader.

Chapter 10

Writing for Martians

Many writers who understand the use of active verbs, economy, and readability make a critical error: They assume the reader knows everything they do. Especially when we write about nontechnical subjects, we assume readers maintain a certain knowledge and experience level. Analyzing your audience members will equip you to address them at their level of understanding. Try this humorous exercise to test all those things we take for granted.

Exercise:

Pretend that a Martian spaceship has landed in your backyard. The Martians need food and you suggest that they make some peanut butter and jelly sandwiches, a human staple. Write a set of instructions for the Martians, assuming they know nothing of peanut butter, jelly, or bread, and describe to them how to make a sandwich. Remember, the Martians do not have the knowledge that you do.

Possible Answer:

Follow a human to the kitchen where we consume our sandwiches. You will find various food substances stored in this kitchen. Ask a human for four items: a loaf of bread, a knife, a jar of peanut butter, and a jar of jelly. The bread, peanut butter, and jelly will have labels stating the name of the product. The knife is an eating implement used to place the peanut butter and jelly on the bread.

Now, we're ready to make sandwiches.

1. Take two pieces, called slices, of bread from the loaf or container of bread.

2. Place them on a horizontal surface.

3. Open the jar of peanut butter by twisting off the lid or top.
4. Take the knife or eating implement and place the thinner end in the jar of peanut butter.
5. Put an amount of peanut butter on the knife and transfer it to one of the slices of bread.
6. Spread the peanut butter from the knife to the bread.
7. Now, open the jar of the jelly.
8. In the same manner, place the thinner end of the knife into the jar of jelly.
9. Put an amount of jelly on the knife and transfer it to the other slice of bread.
10. Take one slice of bread and put in on top of the other slice with the peanut butter or jelly side down.
11. Prepare to enjoy your first sandwich.

A visual or diagram might work well as you try to describe the process. This example might seem ridiculous, yet if you don't know what a knife is, you would have difficulty using one. Likewise, if you describe a process or give a set of instructions for some computer software and the reader can't turn the computer on, your instructions hold no value for that reader.

Master Process Writing

Process writing sounds technical and difficult, but it involves simply presenting a set of instructions or a description of a process to your readers. Most process writing includes a descriptive overview and a set of instructions. User's manuals are examples of process writing. They usually start with a description of a process and then provide detailed instructions for how to use a product—a VCR or a microwave oven, for example.

Exercise:

Try describing in five minutes (time yourself) a process you complete every day, like "getting ready in the morning" or "accessing my voice mail messages."

_____

_____

_____

_____

_____

_____

_____

_____

_____

_____

_____

_____

_____

Could others use your description or set of instructions to complete the project themselves?

When your purpose is to teach or instruct, you probably will use process writing. The most important principle to remember is that readers may or may not have your knowledge of and experience with the topic. Process writing consists of two main parts—an overall description and a set of instructions. Let's talk about descriptive writing first.

Writing Clear Descriptions

Writing a descriptive overview is similar to brainstorming. To describe something, we must know and understand it. Then we can use various techniques to stimulate descriptive phrases. Follow the process of descriptive writing in the next exercise to brainstorm _spring,_ one of the four seasons, in various ways. According to business writing author Michael Keene, you can use 10 or 12 different techniques to create descriptions. This exercise uses six of his brainstorming techniques.

Exercise:

Using the different brainstorming techniques, write a description of the concept of *spring*.

1. **Formal dictionary-like definition:** One of four seasons, spring follows winter and leads into summer; it is the season of rebirth.

2. **Accumulation of detail:** In spring the birds return north from the south, flowers and grasses bloom, trees flower and become green, various animals give birth, temperatures moderate.

3. **Process:** One of the two times of year when the sun crosses the celestial equator and when the lengths of day and night are approximately equal.

4. **Elimination:** Spring is unlike winter when it becomes colder; it is unlike summer, which is drier and hotter; it is unlike fall when leaves fall off the trees in preparation for winter.

5. **Compare/contrast:** Spring is most like autumn, a transitional season leading into a more extreme weather pattern; it is unlike the extreme seasons of winter and summer.

6. **Analogy:** Spring is a time of rebirth when everything comes alive again, like a reawakening or resurrection.

Now, try your hand at the concept of *software*.

1. Formal dictionary-like definition: _____

_____

_____

2. Accumulation of detail: _____

_____

_____

3. Process: _____

_____

_____

4. Elimination: _____

_____

_____

5. Compare/contrast: _____

_____

_____

6. Analogy: _____

_____

_____

Possible Answers:

1. The programming used to run a computer.
2. Software programs include graphics, word processing, and spreadsheet packages.
3. Programmers group together binary information and design commands to make a computer run.
4. Software is not hardware or firmware.
5. Software is like the instructions that make other machines run, but not like the machines or hardware it is used on.
6. An analogy is a road map: When you use a road map, you can find your way through the highway system; when you use software, you negotiate through the computer jungle.

You might be able to write descriptively without using any brainstorming techniques, but some of us need the extra start-up exercise. Once you're in the descriptive mood, you can write an overview or introduction to any process. Next, you must work on writing clear, understandable sets of instructions.

Writing User-Friendly Instructions

Most readers find compact paragraphs of italicized instructions tedious. They're likely to toss them aside to try the process themselves. For example, most people who can program a VCR have never read the instruction manual. They call their friends for advice or figure it out without the hard-to-read instructions.

Use bullet points, headings, or numbers to outline the steps for your reader. The important point to keep in mind is that readers may not understand what you describe. Don't assume everyone knows what you do!

Writing instructions requires left-brain or logical thinking. (Researchers note that the right side of the brain is the seat of creative thinking.) After you present the overview, present the data in a logical, sequential order. Draft the instructions and then review them. Replace any long phrases with shorter ones. Move verbs to the beginnings of sentences. Eliminate every word you can. Remove negative commands like, "When you put paper in the copier, don't try stacking more than 150 sheets." Instead, use a positive statement like, "Stack up to 150 sheets of paper in the copier." If your directions are complex, group the steps into clusters of related points and give them a heading.

According to Susan Perloff, a Philadelphia writer, it's important to have sympathy for your readers. Remember the frustration of trying to put together a bicycle or change a cartridge in a laser printer while reading an allegedly English-written manual? You must be precise, clear, and thorough in your instructions.

According to a study conducted at the University of Rochester in 1992, following directions is gender-based. While men drive by counting mileage or going north, women use landmarks like gas stations to get to a destination. The study of male and female rats in a maze indicated that females depended on landmarks while males depended on vectors or direction.

Let's try an example. Explain to someone who has never tried withdrawing money from an Automated Teller Machine (ATM) how to take $100 from her account. First we'll write a descriptive overview and then a set of instructions.

Example:

Withdrawing Money from an ATM Machine

Description

In the 1980s, banks devised a way to make getting your own money from your bank easier—the ATM machine. These money access machines provide convenient, 24-hour access to your accounts. The bank issues an ATM card and you select a four-digit access number or code that you share with the bank. With this card, you can access your money through a number of ATM machines located not only at banks but also at convenience stores, airports, casinos, etc.

Some ATM machines are equipped with braille plates so blind users can access their monies as well. Some people fear that taking money out in public areas can produce dangerous results. Many ATM machines use cameras to deter robberies.

You can conduct various transactions on an ATM machine, including withdrawals, deposits, and transfers. You can also request an account balance. Read on for exact instructions on how to use these convenient machines.

Instructions

First, decide whether you will drive up to or walk up to an ATM machine. Once you've approached the machine, follow these easy instructions.

1. Insert your card in the manner indicated. The machine will tell you, for instance, to insert your card with the black stripe down and to the right. If you don't enter your card correctly, it will come back to you.

2. After you enter your card, the machine will prompt you for your four-digit code. Enter the code by pressing the number keys on the keypad, then press enter. If you make a mistake, press the clear key and start again. Caution: If you enter the wrong code more than twice, the machine might take or "eat" your card.

3. Once the machine approves your code, it will ask you what transaction you wish to perform. Indicate by pressing the identified key that you would like to make a withdrawal, then press the Enter key.

4. The machine will ask you from which account you would like to withdraw money. Press the key for your primary checking account, then press Enter.

5. The next screen typically asks how much money you would like. Often it lists different dollar amounts, so you can select one and then press Enter. Note: The machine does-n't give coins and often gives only $20 bills.

6. Indicate that you would like $100 and press Enter. The machine will tell you to wait.

7. The money will be issued through a slot in the machine; you'll probably receive five $20 bills.

8. The machine will then ask if you would like another trans-action. Indicate "No."

9. The machine will issue a receipt that usually includes the amount of your withdrawal and the remaining amount in your account.

10. Take your receipt and don't forget to take your card!

These instructions may seem simplistic, but remember that your reader has never used this machine. The true test of a good set of instructions is to allow a novice to try them and see what happens. If he flawlessly takes out $100, your instructions work well. If he can't insert his card properly, you need to review your instructions. Now it's your turn to write a description and set of instructions.

Exercise:

Write a description and set of instructions for pumping your own $10 worth of gas. Remember to explain each step in detail.

_____

_____

_____

_____

_____

_____

_____

_____

_____

_____

_____

_____

_____

_____

_____

_____

Possible Answer:

Pumping Your Own Gas

In many states, you may not pump your own gas. However, in states where it is permitted, pumping your own gas saves money. Most service stations offer the choice of self or full service. Each pump has different options, but in general you can follow the easy instructions displayed at each pump.

Try these easy steps to pump your own gas.

1. Drive into the service station and approach the pump with the fuel tank filler tube on your car on the side closest to the pump. Turn off your engine.

2. Extinguish any cigarettes, cigars, or pipes.

3. Open the fuel door and slowly remove the gas cap, keeping it handy.

4. Check to see if you should prepay or pump first.

5. Decide how you will pay—With a credit card or cash? At the pump or inside?

6. The screen on the pump will prompt you with choices. Select cash outside as your option.

7. Select the octane level you would like. (The cheapest is usually 87.)

8. Follow any instructions on the pump when removing the gas nozzle to place it in your tank. Sometimes you must raise a lever on the pump to start the gas flow.

9. Insert the nozzle from the pump into your gas filler tube. Sometimes you must push the nozzle in to start the gas flowing. Squeeze the trigger in the handle of the nozzle to start the gas flow and hold it to continue to pump gasoline.

10. Watch the pump readout to see how many gallons you're pumping and how much money it is registering. When the monetary amount reads $9.75, start to slowly release pressure on the trigger to slow the pump; add little spurts of gas until the readout says $10.00.

11. Take the nozzle out of the gas filler tube and return it to the pump. Replace the gas cap on your vehicle.

12. Pay the cashier $10.00.

13. Restart your car and drive away.

Did you notice that in both of the examples we indicated possible trouble areas for the reader? Did you notice how clear we were in explaining some of the steps? The overview provided a general description of the process, but did not feature step-by-step instructions. The instructions themselves were step-by-step, numbered items.

Visuals work extremely well with sets of instructions. In the following exercise indicate what type of visual you would suggest to accompany the user's manual or set of instructions.

Exercise:

Indicate what visual you would use in each circumstance.

1. Accessing an ATM machine.

_____

_____

2. Pumping your own gas.

_____

_____

3. Making a peanut butter and jelly sandwich.

_____

_____

4. How to operate a microwave oven.

_____

_____

5. How to change a tire on your car.

_____

_____

6. How to walk a dog.

_____

_____

Most of you probably indicated some type of visual that would make a complicated process easier to explain. For example, drawings of how to put the peanut butter and jelly sandwich together should make it much easier for the Martians!

Now that you've experienced writing overall descriptions and sets of instructions and placing visuals appropriately, let's try combining these skills to produce a mini user's manual. Select the topic you know best and draft a descriptive overview and a set of instructions, indicating where you would place chosen visuals.

Exercise:

Write a mini user's manual on one of the following topics:

How to apply fingernail polish
How to prepare coffee in the morning
How to drive a stick-shift car
How to rollerblade
How to juggle

_____
_____
_____
_____
_____
_____
_____
_____
_____
_____
_____
_____
_____
_____
_____
_____
_____
_____
_____
_____
_____

Test your user's manual out on a friend; see if she or he can perform the process using your guidelines. If so, celebrate; if not, consult the following checklist.

Checklist: Writing for Martians

- Never assume the reader knows what you do.
- Use brainstorming techniques to write descriptively.
- Write concrete, clear sets of instructions, as if you're writing for Martians.
- Use visuals liberally to help explain the process.
- Indicate caution or trouble spots the reader may encounter.

Do's and Don'ts—
The Final Checklist

In this *Quick Guide*, we've discussed how to make your writing more readable, how to design appropriate structures and styles, and how to write for certain situations, such as delivering bad news.

If you remember only one key tip, it should be to keep the reader in mind to write more effectively! This chapter-by-chapter "p.s." will serve as your final checklist for writing well in school or in business.

Chapter One

DO: Know your audience.
DON'T: Assume your audience is like you.

DO: Investigate your audience's age, education level, opinions, and values.
DON'T: Forget to find out what your reader knows about your topic.

DO: Identify your audience type.
DON'T: Assume that you should write the same way for everyone.

DO: Find a way to attract a layperson's attention.
DON'T: Bore laypersons with detail.

DO: Focus on procedure for experts.
DON'T: Give experts only bottom-line data.

| **DO:** | Get to the point for an executive audience. |
| **DON'T:** | Explain detail to an executive audience. |

| **DO:** | Realize that users might not know what you do. |
| **DON'T:** | Be too brief for user audiences. |

| **DO:** | Adjust your tone, vocabulary, and style for each audience type. |
| **DON'T:** | Forget who you're writing to. |

| **DO:** | Figure out your Fog Index. |
| **DON'T:** | Write at a level too high or too low for your audience. |

| **DO:** | Use a "you" or "reader" attitude. |
| **DON'T:** | Get so caught up in what you, the writer, want to say that you lose the reader. |

| **DO:** | Use reader benefits to attract attention. |
| **DON'T:** | Use long paragraphs to draw the reader in. |

| **DO:** | Remember that all readers want to know what's in it for them. |
| **DON'T:** | Use the "me" or "writer" attitude. |

| **DO:** | Use nonsexist language. |
| **DON'T:** | Use he/she—try the plural, they. |

Chapter Two

| **DO:** | Select your one overriding purpose. |
| **DON'T:** | Try to accomplish several purposes in one letter. |

| **DO:** | Use the four steps of the writing process. |
| **DON'T:** | Skip planning and revising—two critical steps in the writing process. |

| **DO:** | Write for quantity in the planning and writing stages. |
| **DON'T:** | Forget to provide quality through revision and editing. |

| **DO:** | Try a five-step revision for longer documents or reports. |
| **DON'T:** | Forget to check for repetitious personal errors like incorrect verb tense or misuse of possession. |

Chapter Three

DO: Use clear, unambiguous language.
DON'T: Use long words if short words will work.

DO: Use specific, precise words.
DON'T: Use complex words that end in *-ality, -ization, -ational*, if you don't have to.

DO: Rephrase unclear sentences.
DON'T: Use words that don't add meaning, like *actually, basically,* and *really.*

DO: Use the 17-word rule when writing sentences.
DON'T: Lose your readers with paragraph-long sentences.

DO: Use economical words.
DON'T: Use wordy phrases, like *with regard to* or *at the earliest possible date,* when you could use *regarding* or *soon.*

DO: Place the subject near the verb for a straightforward order.
DON'T: Use redundancy.

DO: Avoid trite sayings.
DON'T: Use cliches regularly.

DO: Embed negative news in other positive information.
DON'T: Give unnecessary negative news.

DO: Avoid the passive voice.
DON'T: Forget to use active verbs.

DO: Avoid noun and adjective stacks.
DON'T: Use italics and all capital letters liberally.

DO: Make your writing readable.
DON'T: Forget about the "reader" or "you" attitude.

Chapter Four

DO: Use a structure that helps your reader.
DON'T: Forget to use entrance and exit ramps to lure readers and maintain their interest.

DO: Use subject lines and postscripts.
DON'T: Write long-winded first paragraphs.

DO: Use the basic letter format.
DON'T: Forget to use a name or greeting that identifies the reader.

DO: Use electronic manners.
DON'T: Flame people or send spam.

DO: Keep your E-mail messages to one screen.
DON'T: Use all capital letters in your E-mail messages.

DO: Use a standard memo format.
DON'T: Forget to copy appropriate people in your memo.

DO: Use the second person or "you" in memos.
DON'T: Provide endless detail in a memo.

DO: Tell the reader of a direct request how you'll use the information.
DON'T: Forget the reader is usually positive toward your request.

DO: Capture the attention of your audience in informative letters.
DON'T: Forget to embed negative factors in positive material.

DO: State the specific action you want the reader to take in persuasive memos.
DON'T: Fail to use a problem-solution format in persuasive memos.

DO: Send many "good news" letters.
DON'T: Forget that everyone likes to be appreciated.

DO: Present reasons for a "negative news" letter.
DON'T: Forget to reestablish goodwill, if possible.

Chapter Five

DO: Use appealing visuals to attract readers.
DON'T: Neglect the use of white space.

DO:	Use headings every few pages to break the text.
DON'T:	Forget that visuals support text, convey information, and direct action.
DO:	Make your visual accessible for your reader—locate it near the text it belongs with.
DON'T:	Use an inappropriate visual like a pie chart with complex information.
DO:	Make sure you check your visuals for accuracy.
DON'T:	Use tables for simplistic data.
DO:	Use bar graphs to show comparisons between several items.
DON'T:	Use a line graph to show multiple comparisons.
DO:	Use pie graphs to show percentages of a whole.
DON'T:	Forget to use creative visuals like pictographs.
DO:	Use structural visuals for complicated information.
DON'T:	Forget to use photographs to create a mood.
DO:	Use grammatically parallel headings.
DON'T:	Forget to use liberal margins.

Chapter Six

DO:	Use exciting introductions to attract an audience.
DON'T:	Forget to try anecdotes or startling statistics.
DO:	Try CPO introductions.
DON'T:	Forget to use transitions.
DO:	End on a strong note.
DON'T:	Fail to summarize the entire document.
DO:	Always recommend action of some kind in your conclusion.
DON'T:	Forget the impact of the conclusion on the reader.
DO:	Maintain reader interest by using transitions.
DON'T:	Forget to make recommendations or repeat main points in your conclusion.

Chapter Seven

DO: Avoid the overuse of *to be* and *to have*.
DON'T: Rely on a spellchecker; keep a dictionary nearby.

DO: Use active verbs to increase readability.
DON'T: Use cliches frequently.

DO: Know the difference between *i.e.* and *e.g.*
DON'T: Call a corporation or a company *they* instead of *it*.

DO: Make sure each verb agrees in number with its subject.
DON'T: Start a sentence with *There is* or *There are*.

DO: Use the words *lay* and *lie* correctly—*Lie down if you don't feel well* but *Lay the book on the table.*
DON'T: Switch from one verb tense to another unnecessarily.

DO: Make sure your sentence contains a verb and its subject.
DON'T: Punctuate phrases as sentences.

DO: Watch for run-on sentences.
DON'T: Use *it's* as a possessive.

DO: Use parallel structure in headings and subheadings.
DON'T: Use the term *centers around*. (A center is a point.)

DO: Memorize the spelling of irregular plurals like *alumni* and *analyses*.
DON'T: Use *amount* when you mean *number*.

DO: Use *businessperson* rather than *businessman*.
DON'T: Confuse *who* and *whom*.

DO: Proofread everything you write, preferably after you put it aside for awhile.
DON'T: Misuse *I* and *me*. (Use *me* after a preposition and *I* after comparisons.)

DO: Watch your use of collective nouns—generally treat them as singular.
DON'T: Overuse commas.

DO: Use parentheses sparingly.
DON'T: Use the word *irregardless*.

DO:	Use periods for a full stop and semicolons for a shorter stop.
DON'T:	Use redundancies.
DO:	Use apostrophes to show possession.
DON'T:	Use double negatives.
DO:	Use the Gunning-Mueller Fog Index to write at an appropriate level.
DON'T:	Overuse exclamation points.
DO:	Remember to use italics sparingly.
DON'T:	Mistake hyphens for dashes.
DO:	Spell out numbers from zero to ten and all numbers that begin sentences.
DON'T:	Try to impress readers with technical jargon.
DO:	Whenever possible, turn a semicolon into a period and use two separate sentences.
DON'T:	Forget to use a colon after an independent clause to introduce a list.
DO:	Use a dash much like a comma, to pause or to set off a thought that is loosely connected to the sentence.
DON'T:	Use ellipsis points regularly.
DO:	Double check everything for personal grammar errors.
DON'T:	Assume the reader knows everything you do.

Chapter Eight

DO:	Use active verbs.
DON'T:	Write passively.
DO:	Use Subject-Verb-Object order.
DON'T:	Lose the authority of active language.
DO:	Use verbs instead of nouns.
DON'T:	Use cumbersome noun writing.
DO:	Remember passive writing is dull and cumbersome.
DON'T:	Bury the action of your sentence in a noun.

Chapter Nine

DO: Present reasons for negative news.
DON'T: Fail to present any positive aspects.

DO: Try not to offend your reader.
DON'T: Send insulting or threatening communications.

DO: Cast negative news in the most positive possible light.
DON'T: Share unnecessary negative news, like your recent layoff.

DO: Learn techniques for addressing a hostile audience.
DON'T: Belittle or talk down to the reader.

Chapter Ten

DO: Analyze your audience to understand its experience level.
DON'T: Assume your reader knows everything you do.

DO: Master process writing.
DON'T: Forget to use clear descriptions and sets of instructions.

DO: Write descriptive overviews.
DON'T: Forget to use illustrations in your instructions.

DO: Brainstorm to write descriptively.
DON'T: Fail to write user-friendly instructions.

DO: Write concrete, clear sets of instructions, as if you're writing for Martians.
DON'T: Forget to use liberal visuals.

DO: Indicate caution or trouble spots in user manuals.
DON'T: Forget to test user manuals or sets of instructions on someone unfamiliar with the process.

p.s.s. Good luck in your writing endeavors!

Index

abstract writing, 93-4
active voice, 36, 115-125
active writing, 36, 115-125
agreement, 94-5
apostrophe, 95
attachments, 47-8
audiences, 3-16
   complex, 6
   executive, 6
   expert, 5
   hostile, 11, 13, 136-7
   layperson, 5
   mixed, 7
   user, 6

bar graphs, 65-71
body, 47

capital letters, 37
clarity, 26
cliches, 34-5
closings, 47-8
colons, 103
commas, 95-7, 103
complaint letters, 136-7
conclusions, 87-92
cover letters, 58-9
CPO method, 82-6

dashes, 103
date, 46-7
descriptions, 140-3
direct request letters, 51-54

economy, 27-8
editing, 20
ellipsis points, 103
e-mail, 48-51
   etiquette, 50-1
entrance ramps, 45-6
exclamation points, 99
exit ramps, 45-6

fog index, 9-11, 99

good news letters, 59-60
graphs, 65-71
   bar graphs, 65-71
   line graphs, 66, 68-9
   pie graphs, 69-71
   pictographs, 69, 72

headings, 46-7, 68-72
hyphens, 99-100

informative letters, 54-6
inside address, 47
instructions, 140, 143-8
introductions, 82-6
italics, 37, 100

jargon, 35, 100

Latin usage, 100

letters, 51-62
  cover, 58-9
  direct request, 51-54
  good news, 59-60
  informative, 54-6
  negative news, 60=62
  persuasive, 56-8
line graphs, 66, 68-9
linking verbs, 100-101

"me" attitude, 38
memos, 48-51
misused words, 97-9
modifiers, 101

negative news letters, 60-2
negative writing, 35, 60-2, 129-137
nonsexist language, 14-16
nonstandard language, 101
noun writing, 124-5
number style, 101

parallel construction, 102
parentheses, 103
passive voice, 36, 115-125
passive writing, 36, 115-125
periods, 103
persuasive letters, 56-8
pictographs, 69, 72
pie graphs, 69-71
planning, 19
postscripts, 46-7
process writing, 140-150
punctuation, 102-5
  apostrophe, 95
  colons, 103
  commas, 95-7, 103
  dashes, 103
  ellipsis points, 103
  exclamation points, 99
  hyphens, 99-100
  parentheses, 103
  periods, 103
  quotation marks, 103

purpose, 17-9
  document/record, 18
  inform, 18
  persuade, 17
  teach, 18-9

quotation marks, 103

readability, 25-41
redundancy, 32-4, 105
representational visuals, 74
revision, 20-3

salutation, 47
sexist language, 14-6
spelling, 106-9
straightforwardness, 31
structural visuals, 73
subject lines, 46-7
supplement lines, 46-7
SVO order, 121-3

tables, 64-5
transitions, 86-7
trite sayings, 35
typeface, 109

user's manual, 141, 149-150

verbs, 110
  linking verbs, 100-101
visuals, 63-75, 148

white space, 68
who vs. whom, 110
wordiness, 28-30

"you" attitude, 11